PRACTICAL
sewing techniques

PRACTICAL
sewing
techniques

RUTH SLEIGH-JOHNSON

PHOTOGRAPHS BY
MARTIN PALMER

A & C BLACK • LONDON

Acknowledgements

Thank you to all those who allowed their work to be reproduced in this book.

Special thanks to Janine and Charlotte for all the sewing and to models Jasmine and Vianney.

First published in Great Britain 2011
A&C Black Publishers
36 Soho Square
London W1D 3QY
www.acblack.com

ISBN: 978-14081-2748-3

Page design: Susan McIntyre
Cover design: Sutchinda Rangsi Thompson
Publisher: Susan James
Managing editor: Davida Saunders
Copy editor: Alison Wormleighton

Photographs by Martin Palmer, unless otherwise stated

Typeset in: 11 on 14.5pt Celeste

This book is produced using paper that is made from wood grown in managed, sustainable forests. It is natural, renewable and recyclable. The logging and manufacturing processes conform to the environmental regulations of the country of origin.

Printed and bound in China

Publisher's note: Every effort has been made to ensure that the information in this book is accurate. Due to differing conditions, tools, materials and individual skills, the publisher cannot be held responsible for any injuries, losses and other damages resulting from the use of information in this book.

FRONTISPIECE: Skirt made by Chanelle Edwards.

Contents

1 Introduction to sewing techniques

THIS IS A BOOK FOR THOSE WHO SEW ALREADY – and those who have a sewing machine in its case just waiting to be used. The contents of this book have been carefully considered so that you will find in it all that you need, without a load of information that you will never use. It is intended to be not an encyclopedia of sewing but a practical companion for all your projects, whether creative ones or necessary mending and altering tasks.

Often successful sewing is a question of self-belief, and if you follow the step-by-step instructions it will soon become clear that working with fabric, a sewing machine and a needle and thread really isn't difficult. Gaining confidence in the sewing skills and techniques makes for a growing creativity – and it then becomes difficult to put the sewing machine away!

If you are a beginner, you will find the simple construction methods, illustrated with photographs and drawings, all that you need to start transforming fabric, whether you want to create a garment, an accessory or something gorgeous for the home.

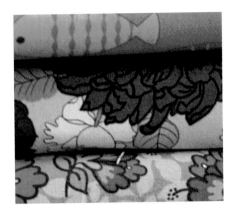

Starting any project is the hardest part, and there are so many techniques to become familiar with that it can seem a bit daunting at first. One good tip for success is to enjoy experimenting. The finished outcomes are going to vary, but all the learning is done by doing.

Begin by kitting yourself out with all that you need. Before you do anything else, go shopping for fabrics. Once you have some lovely fabric, you will be inspired to get started. Which fabrics to choose will depend, of course, on what you have in mind to make. There is a basic fabric guide in this book to point you in the right direction, so try to be practical in your choices. Before deciding, obtain small samples of different colours and textures, patterns and plains, as well as an assortment of trims, buttons and braids to allow you to experiment.

PHOTO BY RUTH SLEIGH-JOHNSON

BASIC EQUIPMENT

Scissors are essential. Cutting shears are used for cutting fabric, and small, pointy embroidery scissors for fiddly jobs. Also handy are dressmaker's scissors and pinking shears.

You will need a **tape measure**, as well as **rulers** 1 m (1 yd), 15 cm (6 in.) and 30 cm (12 in.) long.

Buy a selection of **pins** – the best ones are thin dressmaking pins which won't leave big holes in the fabric.

Needles come in many different sizes and lengths, with eyes of different sizes. The very finest needles are beading needles, and the thickest are for sewing with wool. In between is a range of needles suitable for use with standard thread and with varying fabric thicknesses, which will be fine for sewing through fabrics from cotton to corduroy.

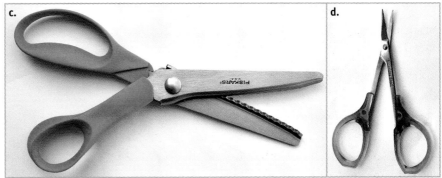
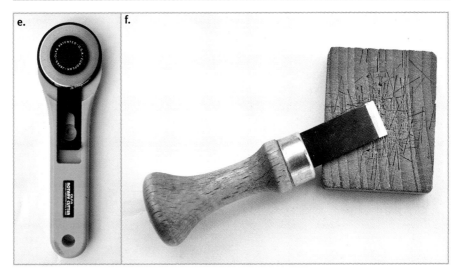
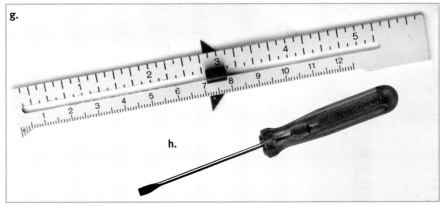

a. Dressmaker's scissors are useful for most jobs.

b. Invest in shears for cutting out fabric.

c. Pinking shears are great for fabric that frays – they give a good edge.

d. Embroidery scissors are an essential.

e. This rotary cutter will be great for cutting out curved or tricky shapes from fabric.

f. This tiny chisel cuts through several layers of fabric, and is a great investment if you are likely to need to make button holes.

g. Accuracy is essential from day one when you are sewing, so a small measure like this is handy to have, as well as a standard ruler and long rule.

h. You will need a small screwdriver whenever you are using a sewing machine.

A magnetic pin catcher saves a lot of time.

For general use, buy a multipack of needles, and select a thin one if you are sewing a fine fabric such as silk, and a thicker one for a fabric such as velvet.

You will use different colours of **thread** in order to match it to the fabric you are using for a project. **Tailor's chalk** or a **fabric pencil** is used for temporarily marking fabric. An **unpicker** comes in handy when you have to unpick seams.

There are numerous other bits and pieces, such as a **needle threader**, **pincushion**, **thimble** and **tweezers**, that you may find useful. Treat yourself to these when you come across them, or put them on your wish list. A sewing box or basket sounds old-fashioned, but there are lots available that are perfect for housing all your tools and that look great, too. Look out for a vintage sewing box – these are often beautifully made.

A SEWING MACHINE

You can make most things by hand, but time is the enemy these days, so a sewing machine is an invaluable piece of equipment. If necessary, you could look out for a reconditioned one or borrow one until you have your own.

When buying, remember that a good-quality machine is an investment. A well-known brand with a good reputation (check consumer reports) should last longer than a cheaper model. It must feature straight and zigzag stitches at the very least, and it is advisable to discuss all the other features with the retailer. A sewing machine is not the best thing to buy online. Instead, test some out in a shop, and ask the experts to show you what they do – it's much easier.

TIP TRY USING A THIN PIECE OF SOAP – THE LITTLE BIT YOU WOULD NORMALLY THROW AWAY – AS A MARKER INSTEAD OF TAILOR'S CHALK OR A FABRIC PENCIL. JUST AS EFFECTIVE, IT WASHES AWAY LEAVING NO STAIN.

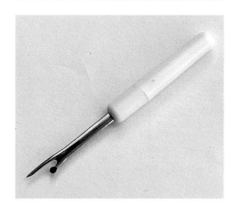

Unpicker, seam ripper, and quick-unpick are different names for the same thing.

Once you have a machine at home, set it up somewhere it can stay out permanently, if at all possible – even if it means eating your dinner off a tray because the dining table is taken over! If the machine is instantly accessible, you will use it all the time, and you'll become good at sewing. If it's out of sight, it's soon going to be forgotten about. So having somewhere to sew is important. Make sure there is enough space for you to do the job efficiently – if necessary, clear the area so that you can sew in comfort.

PRESSING AIDS

Along with sewing, comes pressing. Because everything has to be pressed as it is made, you will need a good clean **iron** and **ironing board**, ideally with a **sleeve board**. Also useful is a **tailor's ham**, which is a fat, padded shape on which you can press awkward bits.

HAPPY SEWING!

Experienced sewers can, with the help of this book, brush up on essential basic techniques and learn some more complex ones. Beginners can learn all the tricks of the trade effortlessly right from the start. With accuracy and care, it is possible to achieve a professional finish and be proud of the results. Making something with your own hands is surprisingly rewarding, and it's also fun to do – so get ready to get making!

This sleeve board is actually two small ironing boards attached one on top of the other. It is used for pressing small or slim areas such as necklines or sleeves.

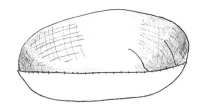

A tailor's ham – a firmly stuffed cushion with rounded ends – is designed for pressing darts, sleeve caps and any area that needs a curved shape pressed.

Gorgeous fabrics can be made into huge floor cushions to brighten any room.

2 Hand sewing

EVEN IF YOU HAVE A SEWING MACHINE, it will still be necessary to do some hand sewing. It isn't at all difficult, and this chapter will soon have you wielding a needle and thread like an expert.

THREADING A NEEDLE

Threading a needle takes patience. Cut a piece of thread about as long as your arm – any longer is hard to sew with. Snip the end off the thread so it is not ragged. Moisten the end of the thread before pushing it through the eye of the needle. Tie a knot, or a few on top of each other, at the end of the long thread that you have pulled through the needle. Do not make a knot that ties the two ends together unless you want a double thickness of thread – this is not needed for most sewing tasks.

A gadget known as a needle threader comes in most sewing kits; give it a try if you find threading tricky. The threader is a thin metal loop that you push through the eye of the needle. The thread is put through the loop and the loop is then pulled back through the needle, leaving the needle complete with thread.

RUNNING STITCH AND TACKING

Running stitch is a straight stitch that is quick to sew. It can be used as a permanent feature, in which case it needs to be sewn neatly and evenly. Or it can be used for tacking, to hold two pieces of fabric together temporarily, until they are sewn together properly with a machine stitch. Tacking can consist of fairly long, uneven stitches, as they will be removed when they are no longer needed and so don't need to look good.

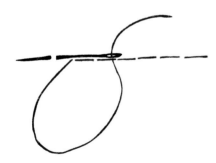

Bringing the needle up from the back of the work, pull the thread through the fabric until the knot prevents you from pulling any further. Determine the length of the stitch by placing the tip of the needle where you want the stitch to end. Stab the needle through the fabric, from the front of the fabric through to the back.

Repeat the process by again bringing the needle up from the back. When the tip of the needle peeps through the fabric, you will see whether the start of the stitch is in the right place, so the stitch will be the same length as the previous one. If it isn't, remove it and try again. If the fabric is not too thick, you can speed things up by inserting the point of the needle in and out several times before pulling the needle and thread through.

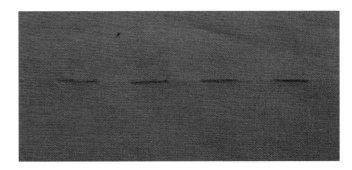

Tacking stitch is a long running stitch – using a contrasting colour makes it easier to see when you remove it.

TAILOR'S TACKS

These are stitches that are used as markers on the fabric instead of chalk markings. They are useful because the stitches can be removed once they have been used to line up the pieces, leaving no marks on the fabric. Tailor's tacks are made using a double length of thread, usually in a contrasting colour that shows up well. Do not knot the ends.

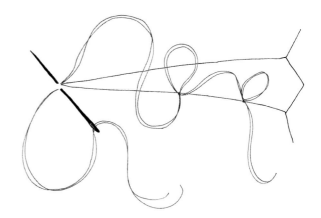

Take a small stitch through both the pattern and the fabric (it can be two layers if you are cutting two identical pieces at once), leaving thread ends 1.5 cm (⅝ in.) long. Make a second stitch in the same place, leaving a loop of thread 3 cm (1¼ in.) long.

After doing all the tailor's tacks needed in an area, such as on a dart, nip the thread to leave ends 1.5 cm (⅝ in.) long, and snip through the middle of the loop.

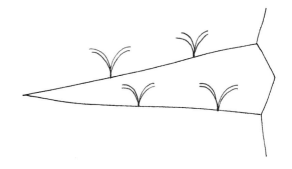

Carefully pull the pattern away without pulling the threads out of the fabric. If there are two layers of fabric, separate these and snip the tailor's tacks between the layers so that tufts of thread are left in each layer.

BACKSTITCH

This looks like a running stitch but without gaps between the stitches. It is useful for making durable hand-stitched seams if you do not have a sewing machine. Start from the back of the fabric every time you sew, so that the knot will not show.

Bringing up the needle from the back of the work, pull the thread through the fabric until the knot prevents you from pulling any further.

Determine the length of the stitch by placing the tip of the needle where you want the stitch to end. Stab the needle through the fabric, from the front of the fabric through to the back.

Bring your needle up from the back of the work through to the front, at the point where you want the stitch to end – where the needle comes through the fabric will determine the length of the stitch.

Bring the thread from the front of the work to the back, by inserting the needle just next to the place where the first stitch ends.

To make the third stitch, bring the thread through at the place where the second stitch ends. Continue to repeat the process.

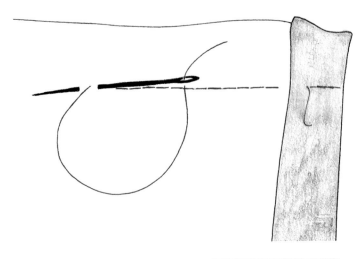

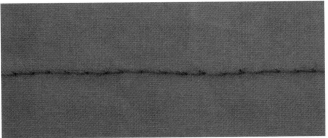

Backstitch is a strong stitch – it looks like this.

BLANKET STITCH

This stitch is a decorative stitch, perfect for finishing raw edges of garments, or on any fabric edge that is not hemmed. Blanket stitch also looks great on patches and appliqué. Wool or embroidery silks work well – the stitches are supposed to stand out – and contrasting colours draw attention to the stitching. To do this stitch successfully, keep the thread loose as you are working.

Bring the thread through from the back of the fabric to the front. In one continual motion, take the needle over the fabric edge and around to the back of the fabric again. Bring the thread through from the back of fabric to the front a second time, about 5 mm (¼ in.) to the right of the previous stitch, using the tip of the needle to loop through the stitch.

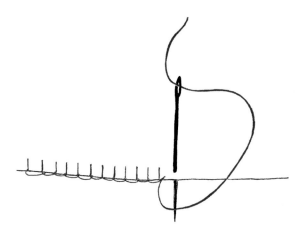

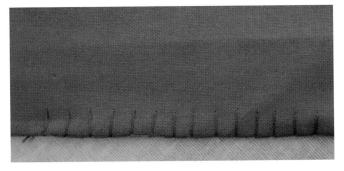

Blanket stitch makes a decorative edge and also helps prevent the fabric from fraying.

INVISIBLE HEM

This is a way of stitching a hem without the stitches showing on the front of the fabric. First pin and tack the hem in place.

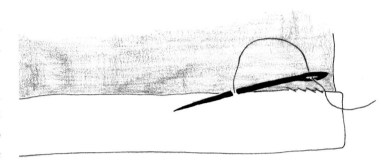

Bringing your needle up from the back of the work, pull the thread through the fabric until the knot prevents you from pulling any further. Make a tiny stitch – no more than a dot – on the top of the fabric and take the thread through to the back of the fabric.

Make a longer stitch on the back of the fabric, where it will not show, before bringing the thread through to the top and making another tiny, nearly invisible stitch.

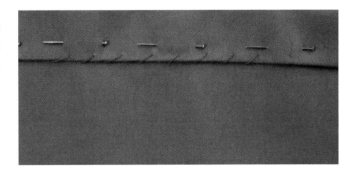

Slip stitch (see p.54) is formed in much the same way as invisible hemming, but you don't have to be quite so careful about taking only a tiny thread from the top of the fabric.

DARNING

The thread you use for darning needs to match the fabric, so use the same colour and also the same texture – for example, use wool on a woollen jumper. Work darning on the wrong side of the fabric.

On a weak area that has not yet become a hole, make stitches in one direction across the width of the weak area of fabric. Now weave the thread through that stitching at right angles to it, making tiny stitches at the beginning and end of each of these lines, to create a woven patch of tiny stitches.

To darn a hole, trim the jagged edge as it will be easier to darn a neat edge. Do not cut off an unnecessary amount of fabric – the smaller the area, the less it will show.

Machine darning is, of course, much quicker. Drop the feed dog on the machine as you would for machine embroidery stitching, and work over the area to be darned with a backwards and forwards motion to build up a layer of stitches.

Begin a good distance away from the hole in order to reinforce the thin fabric around it. Sew stitches that span the hole from one side to the other, close together. Turn the work 90 degrees, and weave under and over the thread. Repeat this process to build up a layer of crosswise and lengthwise stitches to form a patch that will become stronger as the layer thickens.

MENDING A SPLIT SEAM

Turn the seam so that you are looking at the inside of the garment or item and can identify exactly where the stitching stops and the seam is open. With the edges of the seam together, make short running stitches by hand in a straight line, from just before the place where the stitches stop until you are stitching along where the seam resumes. (These stitches on top of the original stitching are just to add strength.) You can use a machine stitch to do the same, and these smaller, more uniform stitches will give a more durable seam.

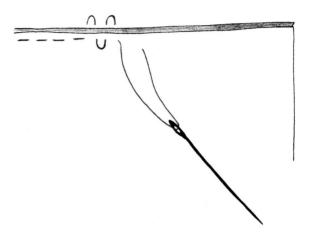

Make sure the new stitching exactly follows the seam line.

PATCHING A RIP

You will need to decide whether to use an inconspicuous patch that matches the fabric, or to make a feature of the patch using completely different fabric. Either way, the patch must be larger than the hole. It is sensible to use worn fabric or wash the fabric before using it for patching.

For a feature patch, you could sew the patch on top of the garment or item on the right side, finishing the edge with blanket stitch or running stitch. On trousers you will need to be careful not to sew through both sides of a leg. However, on garments or items where you can easily sew through just one layer of fabric, you could use a machine zigzag stitch to attach the patch as a piece of appliqué.

Alternatively, place the patch of fabric right side up on the inside of the garment or item, underneath the area to be patched, which will usually be a rip or hole. If the tear is jagged it will look better if it is trimmed first. Hand tack the patch in place so it is fully covering the worn area. Using a small, neat hemming stitch, hand sew the patch to the underside of the hole or worn area. On the right side of the patched area, work a row of stitching around the edge of the rip or hole, close to it, to ensure the patch stays firmly in place. You could make this a decorative feature by using contrasting thread or even thick thread such as embroidery silk.

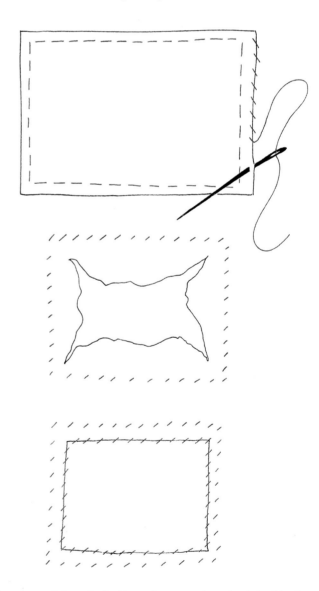

You can patch from the inside or place a patch on the right side of the fabric.

USING VELCRO AND FUSIBLES

This is a quick way of fastening two hemmed edges. Pull the two strips of Velcro apart. Pin one of the strips to the underside of one hemmed edge, and the corresponding strip to the right side of the other hemmed edge. Stitch each strip in place by hand or machine, in two straight lines – one at the top edge of the Velcro and one at the bottom edge.

To hem a garment, curtains or any edge without a single stitch, buy fusible webbing, which is ironed in place. The heat of the iron fuses the layers together as though they were glued – which they are in a sense, as fusible webbing is a tape that has an adhesive on both sides.

FANCY FRAYING

Edges can be carefully frayed as an alternative way of finishing the edges. Simply use a pin or needle to tease out and remove the threads that are parallel to the edge, leaving a fringe formed from the crosswise threads.

SEWING ON BUTTONS

Buttons add impact, and knowing how to sew them on is an essential sewing skill, whether you are making a new garment or cushion or simply sewing on a button that has fallen off. On an item you already have, a complete change of buttons can alter the look dramatically, making a cheap item look classy, or a dull item more interesting.

Find the spot where the button was attached or decide where the button should go. On a garment or item you're making, to ensure that buttons are lined up properly with the buttonholes, overlap the closing and pin it closed. Poke a pin through each buttonhole to mark where the buttons need to be sewn. Make sure that the pins are all the same distance from the edge. Mark the position of each button with tailor's chalk.

Fasten a safety pin through the exact spot where you will sew on the button. The pin will act as a spacer between the fabric and the button while you are sewing.

Thread your needle with a double length of thread that matches (or contrasts with) the button. Tie a double or treble knot at the end.

Insert the needle from the back of the fabric, up through the button and pull it and the thread all the way through. Push the button against the fabric. Now insert the needle down through another hole in the button to the back of the fabric. Stitch from hole to hole in a way that will create a neatly sewn on button. Continue sewing up and down through the holes until the button is securely attached. Remove the safety pin.

Bring the thread through to the front of the fabric under the button, winding tightly around the stitches under the button to form a thread shank. Now take the needle down through the fabric and fasten off. (On a heavy garment such as a coat, you will need to make the thread shank about as deep as your little finger. After you have about eight to ten threads between the button and the fabric, stitch loops over and over these threads to create a stiff shank.)

If the button has a metal shank rather than holes in the button itself, sew through the fabric and shank with small stitches at right angles to the buttonhole to keep the button in place. Fasten the thread on the wrong side with several stitches.

  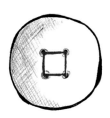

A choice of ways to sew on a button: choose the one you prefer.

3 Using a sewing machine

A SEWING MACHINE IS PRETTY MUCH ESSENTIAL for anyone wanting to sew. It saves you an enormous amount of time – once you have mastered how to use it! It also gives you consistent stitches that are stronger than hand stitches, as it is looping two threads together to form the stitch.

It may be that you are using a sewing machine that you have had for ages or that you are borrowing a friend's, but if you are hoping to buy one, take your time. Choosing a sewing machine is a task that you need help with. Ask around first – your sewing friends may be able to recommend a machine that they find really good. Research and compare prices online to give you an idea of what is on offer in the marketplace before taking the next step. Then go and try the machines for yourself to see them in action.

Your best bet is a shop that specialises in sewing machines so that an expert can demonstrate different machines for you. Buying from a specialist shop or department means you can also have some basic tuition to help you set up and use the machine. Some shops provide free tutorials or a course of classes that you pay for, so you become an expert yourself.

Straight and zigzag stitching are the bare essentials, but, in fact, all modern machines will do a variety of decorative stitches as well. Lots of machines have numerous features and gadgets, such as needle threaders and thread cutters. Also useful is the ability to adjust the needle position. Another feature worth looking out for is a button that you can press to instruct the needle to stop in either the 'up' or the 'down' position. This is handy for pivoting around corners and for appliqué work, as it generally gives you more control of the work.

However, if you are working with an older machine without any fancy features, don't worry. You will be able to manage adequately with a machine that just does the basics. You will also probably find that it is more metal than plastic, which makes it more durable – although a lot heavier.

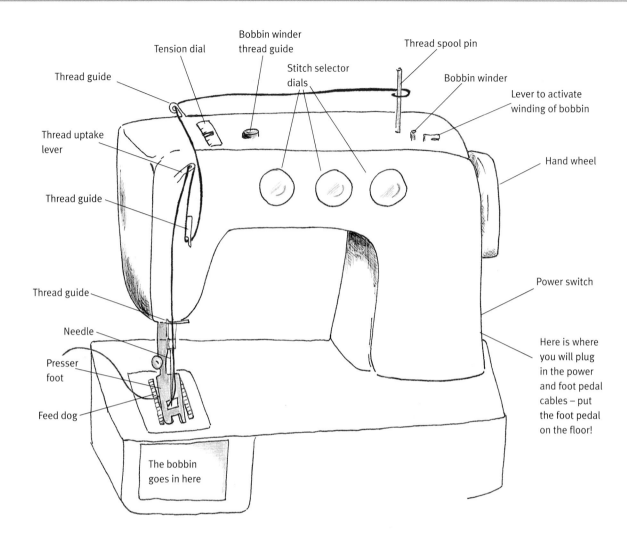

Tension dial

Bobbin winder
thread guide

Thread spool pin

Thread guide

Stitch selector
dials

Bobbin winder

Lever to activate
winding of bobbin

Thread uptake
lever

Hand wheel

Thread guide

Thread guide

Power switch

Needle

Here is where
you will plug
in the power
and foot pedal
cables – put
the foot pedal
on the floor!

Presser
foot

Feed dog

The bobbin
goes in here

HOW IT ALL WORKS

POWER SWITCH Start by plugging the machine in and turning the power switch to the 'on' position.

NEEDLE The shank of the needle is inserted into the machine. It is often flat on the back side, but some are completely round. The shaft of the needle usually has a groove along it. Most machines insert the needle with the front of the needle facing you, while a few have the front of the needle facing left. Large needles with a thick shaft will be stronger, but they will also make a bigger hole in your fabric. A general rule is to use a thin needle for lightweight fabric and a thicker needle for heavier fabric.

To put the needle in or change it, you either turn the knob just above the needle or use a tiny screwdriver (usually supplied with the machine) to undo the screw that holds the needle in place. The needle will then be easy to remove. Put the new one in place with the flat area, if any, in the correct position. Tighten the knob or screw, and you are fit to go!

BOBBIN AND BOBBIN CASE A bobbin is either metal or plastic. A small spool onto which thread is wound, it fits into a bobbin case. The bobbin case can be part of the internal workings of the machine but is most often a separate piece that is then loaded into the machine. Always buy the right bobbins for your machine. Wind thread onto it with care – a badly wound bobbin causes lots of problems.

BOBBIN WINDER This is a short peg on which the bobbin (not in its case) is placed in order for the thread to be wound onto the bobbin. The peg spins the bobbin and in this way it is wound with thread. It has no other use.

BOBBIN WINDER THREAD GUIDE This is the halfway 'hook' for the thread between the spool and the bobbin when the bobbin is on the bobbin winder. It controls the tension of the thread as it fills the bobbin.

THREAD SPOOL PIN The spoke where you put your thread, this usually points straight up but may be horizontal. The little cap that holds the thread on a horizontal pin is easy to lose, whereas you don't have that problem with a vertical spool pin.

THREAD GUIDES There is always a hook on the top of the machine, or occasionally it can be just at the back, in a position that makes it easy to feel. Feel along the top edge of the machine – there's no need to stand up and look for it once you have established where it is. There are usually other guides close to the thread uptake lever and the needle. These hooks keep the thread going in the right direction.

THREAD UPTAKE LEVER This moves up and down as you sew. Turn the wheel towards you or gently press the foot pedal and you will see this happening. The lever will be in the 'up' position when a stitch has been completed, so always try to finish your stitching with this lever in that position.

TENSION DIAL Although the tension dial varies from one machine to another, most have a setting marked with a red line that indicates where the tension is usually ideal. If the tension is wrong you can change the setting on the dial, but the real troubleshooting involves the two metal plates inside the machine and how tightly they are holding the thread in place. Because each machine is different, you will need to consult the manual for how to adjust this all-important part.

STITCH LENGTH SELECTOR Turn this knob to select the stitch length. A short stitch length is secure, while a long stitch (a large number on the dial) is not only longer but also looser. It is good for basting, which is a temporary stitch. A gathering stitch is the longest of all.

'o' length means the stitch does not go forward at all – the needle will go up and down on the spot unless you have set it to do some width-wise

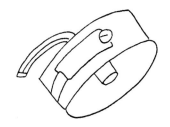

Bobbin case.

Bobbin wound with thread.

movement. You will only use 'o' if you are doing a zigzag stitch that is so close together that it is, in fact, a satin stitch.

STITCH WIDTH SELECTOR A straight stitch has no width – this dial will be set to 'o'. If you want a stitch that goes from side to side – a zigzag stitch – you need to select on this dial how wide the stitch will be.

REVERSE STITCH BUTTON It's handy to be able to reinforce stitches by going over them backwards – press this as you press down the foot pedal to change the direction of your sewing.

PRESSER FOOT This holds the fabric to the feed dog – think of it as a seat belt that you put in place before you drive your machine. A lever at the back of the machine – in an easy 'feeling' position – lifts the foot up (to put the fabric in the machine or to remove it) or down (to sew). There are different types of foot for different purposes (see p.29), such as inserting a zip.

FEED DOG These metal plates located below the presser foot feed the fabric through the machine as you guide it.

FOOT PEDAL Putting pressure on this pedal is like putting your foot on the accelerator in a car; it makes the machine go. If you are a learner driver, don't put your foot down too hard, as it will make the machine go too fast, which is harder to control.

HAND WHEEL This performs the same function as the foot pedal but at a snail's pace. You use this wheel to bring up the bobbin thread when you are setting up the machine, and to move the needle into or out of the work when you have finished stitching – or when the thread is in a muddle. Also use the wheel to control the needle when you are manoeuvring around tricky bits, such as a bead or a button.

THREADING THE MACHINE

FILL THE BOBBIN FIRST

1. Put the empty bobbin on the bobbin winder, and the thread on the thread spool pin.

2. Take the end of the thread from the spool and lead it around the bobbin winder thread guide.

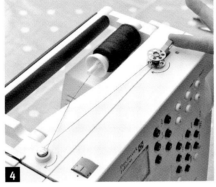

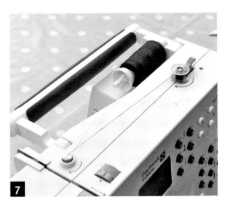

3. Wind a little thread onto the bobbin by hand.

4. Push the bobbin to the action position, or push the lever, depending on the machine model.

5. Disengage the needle's up-and-down action by turning the inner crank on the hand wheel (on older models of machine) or pulling out the hand wheel, or whatever your particular machine does.

6. Depress the foot pedal to start winding.

7. The spinning bobbin winds on the thread.

Gently guide the thread onto the bobbin with one hand as the bobbin spins. Make sure the bobbin is winding evenly, as it will mess up your stitching if it's not. Some machines will automatically stop when the bobbin is full – if yours does not, be careful not to overfill it.

NEXT LOAD THE BOBBIN INTO ITS CASE

Most bobbins load into a separate bobbin case. Think of the case as a hollow apple, which has a stalk.

1. Holding the bobbin so that the thread is going in an anticlockwise direction as you look at it, and the bobbin case so the 'stalk' is pointing upwards, drop the bobbin into the case.

2. Guide the thread to the slit at the side of the case close to the 'stalk'.

3. Guide the thread through the slot and under the plate.

4. The thread will come out of the hole.

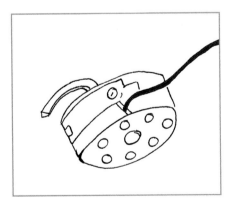

5. Pull the thread through the slit.

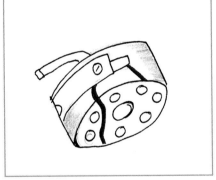

6. Pull the thread under the plate.

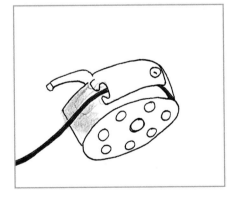

7. The thread comes out here.

8. (Right) Open the little door at the back of the bobbin case. Keep it open as you insert the bobbin case into the machine. It will stop the bobbin from falling out of the case.

9. (Far right) Place the bobbin, in its case, into the machine. Gently press the stalk into the stalk-shaped hole until you hear it click into place.

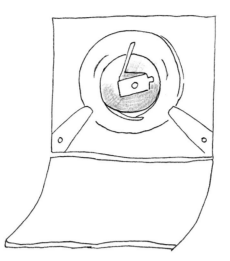

NOW DEAL WITH THE TOP THREAD

This is a general example of the path the thread takes to reach the needle, but it varies from machine to machine.

1. Put the thread on the thread spoke, and along to the first stop: the thread guide.

2. Guide the thread behind the hook.

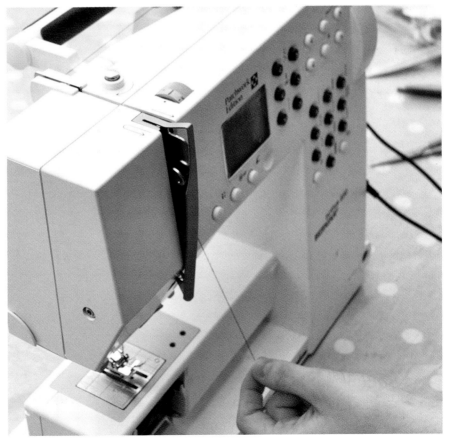

3. Take it down through the thread plates.

4. Next through the uptake lever.

5. Bring the thread down towards the needle.

6. Then through the guides close to the needle.

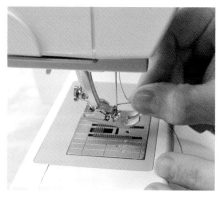

7. Through the thread guide at the top of the needle.

8. Thread it through the needle (usually from front to back).

9. Some machines have a threading device.

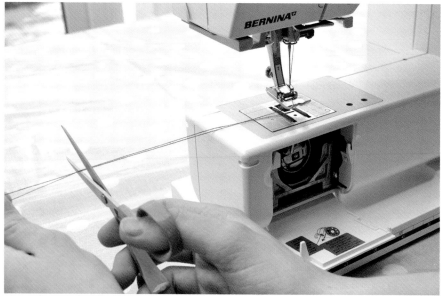

10. Turn the hand wheel to bring the bobbin thread up.

11. Pull the threads long before you cut them. You are ready to sew!

BRINGING UP THE BOBBIN THREAD

With the thread from the sewing machine pulled through the needle, turn the hand wheel towards you. The thread from the bobbin will appear just beneath the presser foot. You might need to gently slide the loop of thread away from the machine to make sure it is fully out – the top thread has brought the bobbin thread to the surface, ready for action. Bring both threads to the back of the machine in preparation for sewing.

ADJUSTING THREAD TENSION

The strength of your stitches depends on using the correct thread tension. If the tension is too loose there is too much thread for the stitch, and if it is too tight there is not enough thread for the stitch. Having the tension too loose will result in the stitches on the underside of the sewing being loopy, and you will be able to see the top thread on the underside of the fabric. If the tension is too tight, the stitching on the underside of the sewing will be taut, and you will be able to see the bobbin thread on the top of the fabric.

The tension dial on the sewing machine controls the top thread, and you can correct the tension of your stitches by adjusting this dial. There is usually a marker to show the normal position of the tension dial, but it may need adjusting to suit different weights and thicknesses of fabric.

If that does not resolve any problems you have with tension, you could adjust the bobbin thread. To do this you have to take out the bobbin case and the surrounding part of the machine, but be sure to read the manual and carefully follow the instructions.

TIP   ALWAYS HAVE THE NEEDLE IN THE WORK AND THE PRESSER FOOT DOWN BEFORE YOU PUT YOUR FOOT ON THE FOOT PEDAL TO START SEWING!

IN A MUDDLE?

If the thread gets in a mess, it could be caused by any of the following:

- The most common cause is the machine not being threaded correctly, so rethreading is the first remedy to try.
- Are you stitching with the presser foot up? It's easily done, but will always cause tangles.
- Check that the bobbin thread is neatly wound – it might be coming to the end of the thread.
- Check the tension – look at the dial first of all and then, if necessary, the whole bobbin case and surrounding part (using the manual).
- Check no one has tampered with the dials.
- Make sure the settings are appropriate for the stitch you want to do.
- The teeth of the feed dog should be in the 'up' position. If they are in the 'down' position, they will not grip the fabric and feed it through.
- Is the needle secure? If not, tighten it. If it has been recently changed, check that it has been inserted correctly.

BEGINNER'S GUIDE TO STITCHING

STITCHING STRAIGHT

Place one hand on each side of the work as you sew. Gently guide the work without pulling it through the machine. Use the guide on the metal plates to help you.

STITCHING CORNERS

Sew along in a straight line. At the point where you want to turn a corner, stop stitching, with the needle down (in the work). Lift the presser foot, with the needle holding the work in place. Pivot the fabric around the needle until it is in position for the next row of stitches. Lower the presser foot and continue sewing.

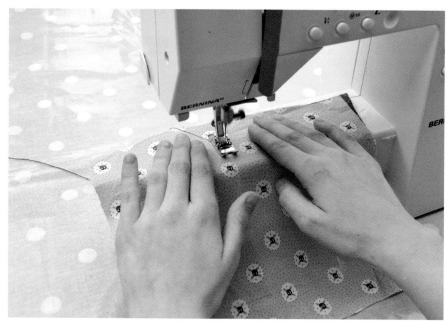

Keep your hands flat but do not press down on the fabric.

STITCHING CURVES

This takes practice. There is no real technique to learn, but draw a curly tailor's chalk line on fabric and try to sew on top of it. After a few attempts, you are bound to see an improvement.

TOPSTITCHING

This is simply machine stitching parallel to an edge or seam, which is done from the right side of the fabric. As well as keeping the edges and seams flat, it emphasises the lines of the garment.

STAY STITCHING

Stitching through a single layer of fabric just inside the seam line on a curved or angled edge (such as a neckline) will help prevent it from stretching before it is seamed. Known as stay stitching, it is done with a straight stitch and a regular stitch length, immediately after the piece has been cut out.

CHOOSING YOUR STITCH

Zigzag stitch gives a finish to edges that helps prevent the fabric from fraying. It is also used to hold a shape of fabric in place when it is being appliquéd to a background fabric. Close-together zigzag stitches form a decorative satin stitch.

Decorative stitches are programmed to work at the flick of a switch on modern machines. They provide finishes for edges as well as decoration on garments and furnishings.

Free machine embroidery is done by using either a straight or a zigzag stitch with the feed dog in the 'down' position, so that the fabric is not being gripped in place. With this freedom, you can guide the fabric around while the stitches create a painterly effect.

CHOOSING YOUR NEEDLE

Needles are available in different sizes to suit fabrics of varying thicknesses. Some are for specific fabrics, such as stretchy fabrics or leather, or are designed for specific purposes, such as decorative topstitching.

The most commonly used needles are the following:

- Sharp-point needles for woven fabrics
- Ballpoint needles for knitted fabrics
- Denim needles for denim and heavy, thick fabrics
- Blue-tip needles for delicate silks and synthetics
- Twin needles for topstitch

A narrow zipper foot is a necessary extra for your sewing machine.

CHOOSING YOUR MACHINE FOOT

There are a number of sewing machine feet, allowing the sewing machine to be used to full advantage, but which feet are available to you depends on your model of sewing machine. A very basic machine may have only a standard all-purpose foot, but if you are able to change the foot on the machine, try doing so. Get familiar with the machine feet that you have!

Apart from the standard all-purpose foot, these are the most useful feet:

Zigzag foot: This all-purpose foot is used for both straight and zigzag stitch.

Zipper foot: This foot allows the needle to stitch close to the zip teeth. There is also a concealed zipper foot specifically for inserting concealed zips.

Embroidery foot: This is a special metal hoop foot which makes machine embroidery more successful.

Buttonhole foot: This is designed for stitching a buttonhole in four steps. The buttonhole is sewn in lines of zigzag stitch that are so close together they look like satin stitch. It is stitched in four stages: a row of stitches at the top; a row to one side; a row on the opposite side; and a row at the bottom. Most machines have a programme that automatically sews the four stages to create a beautifully neat buttonhole for you.

Hemmer foot: Narrow hems are stitched efficiently with this foot.

A hooped foot for freehand embroidery is something you might like to buy as a luxury item. You can only do freehand embroidery using a sewing machine that has a front-loading bobbin which sits in its own bobbin case, not a bobbin that drops in on the top of the machine.

4 Fabrics

FABRICS ARE MADE FROM FIBRES THAT ARE TWISTED together to form yarns, which are then woven or knitted together, or joined in some other way such as bonding, felting or fusing. All these factors influence what a fabric looks like and how it behaves.

FIBRES

Fabrics are made from natural fibres (animal or vegetable sources) or from fibres that are from not grown naturally (either man-made or synthetic), or from a mixture of both.

Wool, from the fleece of sheep or goats, is extensively used for garments, blankets and carpets. It is warm, soft and hard-wearing. **Flannel**, **cashmere** and **mohair** are all types of wool fabric.

Silk, made from the cocoons of silkworms, is used for delicate garments and accessories. It has a wonderful drape and is really soft and comfortable to wear. **Taffeta** and **chiffon** are both fabrics that are often made from silk.

Cotton, from the seed pods of the cotton plant, is the most versatile of fabrics. Used for all kinds of garments, household and furnishing fabrics, it is cool, comfortable, durable and easy to care for. There are many varieties of cotton, ranging from strong **denims** to **towelling** and **velvet**.

Linen, made from the stem of the flax plant, is used as both a fashion and an interiors fabric, used for clothing and furnishings, especially tableware. Although linen creases easily, it has a luxurious quality.

Rayon is made from plant cellulose, which is regenerated to form fibres. It can be made to resemble natural fibres and comes in a range of qualities, from lightweight to heavy, and in different textures. **Viscose** and **acetate** are both rayon.

Synthetic fibres are produced chemically. Durable and crease-resistant but not absorbent, they include **polyester**, **nylon** and **acrylic**, all petrochemical derivatives.

TEXTURE, COLOUR AND PATTERN

As well as different fibres and construction methods, fabrics come in an infinite number of combinations of textures, colours and patterns.

Texture is created by the fibre and the way in which the fabric is constructed. There are endless textures, including laces, metallics, velvets and tweeds. But remember, clingy fabrics reveal, and chunky fabrics add bulk.

Colour is perhaps the most influential factor affecting fabric choice. You will often be drawn to a colour for no particular reason. Colour schemes are important if you are working to make something for the home; think about what else will be in the room and chose a harmonising scheme that is easy to live with, or pick one colour that varies in its value (lightness or darkness). For fashion items go for a colour that will suit both the wearer and the purpose of the garment – for example, white trousers for a child would not stay that way for long!

Patterns come in dots, stripes, floral and retro prints, to name just a few. Again, the questions of what you are making, where it will be used or worn and who it is for will help you narrow down the choices.

Look around you for inspiration when choosing fabric colours – go for lots of shades of one colour (monochrome) or a contrasting colour scheme – you choose!

Source vintage fabric to make clothing, accessories and things for your home. Designs from decades ago are now inspiring contemporary textile designers, so why not find and use the real thing?

PHOTO BY RUTH SLEIGH-JOHNSON

A SELECTION OF FABRICS

WOOL

Crepe: Fine and soft; used for suits and dresses.

Flannel: A strong, soft fabric; used for jackets, skirts and trousers.

Gabardine: A tightly-woven, hard-wearing and comfortable fabric; used for skirts and trousers.

Jersey: A versatile wool; used for casual clothing and children's wear.

SILKS

Chiffon: Soft and good for draping; used for lingerie and blouses.

Dupion: A stiff silk fabric; used for dresses and bridal wear.

Organza: Transparent and mainly used for bridal wear and dance costumes.

Satin: With a luxurious feel to its surface, this is commonly used for special-occasion wear.

COTTON

Chambray: Lightweight and easy to wear; used for shirts, blouses and dresses.

Chintz: Glazed cotton (the surface has had special treatment); used mainly for home furnishings, such as curtains.

Corduroy: Soft, hard-wearing and with a ribbed texture; often used for children's clothes.

Cotton jersey: Comfortable and durable; used for dresses, T-shirts and sportswear.

Cotton lace: Used for tablecloths, curtains and trimming on special-occasion dresses.

Denim: Strong and durable; used for jeans, jackets and work wear.

Gingham: A lightweight checked fabric; used for children's clothes and table linen.

Poplin: A soft and fine-surfaced fabric used for dresses, shirts and blouses.

Seersucker: Treated so it has a puckered texture; used for blouses and dresses.

Towelling: Absorbent and most often used for towels and bathrobes.

Velvet: Hard-wearing and luxurious; used for evening wear, trousers and soft furnishings.

LINEN

Handkerchief linen: Sheer and light-weight; used for hankies and blouses.

Suiting linen: Soft and comfortable to wear; used for skirts, jackets and shirts.

SYNTHETIC

Acetate: A fabric that drapes well and is available in different weights; used for dresses and sportswear.

Acrylic: Can be woven or knitted; resembles wool.

Nylon: Strong and lightweight; used for rain wear and ski wear.

Polar fleece: Soft and warm; used for cosy outer wear, sweatshirts and hooded tops.

Viscose: Soft and hard-wearing; used for dresses and skirts.

5 Construction details

WHETHER YOU ARE MAKING A BAG OR A SHIRT, it is the construction details that will make the fabric actually work for you. To convert the two dimensions of fabric into three dimensions, you are essentially shaping fabric by creating form. This is done with darts, gathers and pleats, which are explained in this section. Seams that curve are another essential ingredient, while facings, interfacings and linings help to keep the shape in place.

SEAMS

A seam is a line of stitches that hold two pieces of fabric together. To stitch a perfect seam, always adjust the machine tension and stitch length to suit the fabric you are working with. If your machine doesn't have a seam guide attachment, make your own by placing a piece of coloured tape 1 cm (⅜ in.), or whatever is the desired width of the seam, from the needle.

There are many types of seam that you can use, and in garment construction especially some more complicated types of seam are recommended. Some are done because they are more practical, while others just look nice, giving a professional finish.

On patterns or in instructions, you will often see that the 'seam allowance' is referred to. This is the measurement of the fabric that extends beyond the stitching line. By creating a seam you therefore 'lose' a little of the fabric. If the seam allowance is, say 1 cm (⅜ in.), then two pieces of fabric sewn together with a seam will measure 2 cm (¾ in.) less in width than when they were laid out flat, side by side, before sewing. Remember to 'allow' for this when you sew. The size of the seam allowance may be specified in the instructions for your garment or item, or you may need to decide the width yourself. In most cases it should be 1–1.5 cm (⅜–⅝ in.).

Before sewing any seam, lay the two pieces of fabric on a flat surface, with the raw edges even. Pin them together, inserting the pins at right angles to the seam line.

Most of the time you can go ahead and stitch the seam using a permanent stitch. However, if you are not certain whether the garment will fit, you might want to use a basting stitch first. Usually done on a machine, basting is simply a temporary stitch. Because it is long and loose, it is easy to undo. If you do this by hand it's normally referred to as tacking (see pp.12–13).

A casing through which a ribbon has been threaded to create a drawstring bag.

Tacking prior to stitching is useful when the seam will be difficult to stitch. Even experienced sewers rely on basting or tacking for an accurate result, but for beginners it is a particularly good idea.

If you haven't used tacking, it's best to remove the pins as you stitch, easing out each one just before you get to it, rather than stitching over them. Even though the presser foot can generally cope with running over pins, you risk breaking a needle and crumpling up the fabric.

PLAIN SEAM

Use this for any regular seam. Pin two pieces of fabric with right sides together and stitch using a straight stitch. Press the seam open.

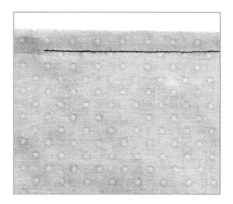 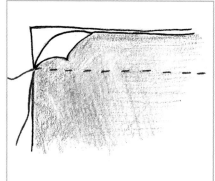

FRENCH SEAM

This is good for sheer fabrics as it leaves no unfinished seam edges. The seam allowance needs to be 1.5 cm (⅝ in.) for this.

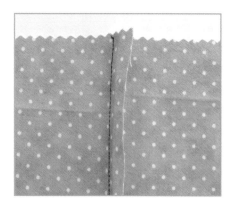 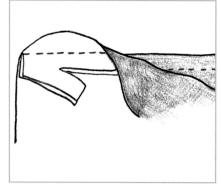 

Place the fabrics with wrong sides together, and stitch a plain seam 5 mm (¼ in.) from the edge.

Trim the seam allowance (also called turnings) to 3 mm (⅛ in.). Turn the fabric so that the right sides are together and press it flat at the seam.

Pin in place before sewing a seam line 1 cm (⅜ in.) from the fold. The first seam is then hidden inside the second seam.

FLAT FELL SEAM

This is a strong and sturdy seam, which is used in manufacturing on garments such as sportswear and pyjamas. It's good for any seam that needs to be particularly durable, but because it is bulky it is not recommended for thick fabric. With a flat fell seam, a line of stitching is visible on the right side parallel to the seam. The seam allowance needs to be 1.5 cm (⅝ in.) for this.

Place the two fabrics with right side together and stitch a 1.5 cm (⅝ in.) plain seam. Press the seam to one side and then trim the lower seam allowance to 3 mm (⅛ in.). Turn under the raw edge of the other seam allowance and wrap it over the trimmed edge. Pin the folded-over seam allowance to the fabric and then stitch close to the folded edge through all four thicknesses.

This is the seam you will see used on jeans as it is hard-wearing.

SLOT SEAM

This is a wonderfully decorative seam, which features a flash of contrasting fabric.

On each of the two pieces of fabric to be joined, fold back the seam allowance and press.

Cut a strip of contrasting fabric about 4 cm (1½ in.) wide and as long as the entire seam. Sew a row of tacking stitches lengthwise down the middle of this strip.

Place the contrasting strip right side up on the work surface, and the two fabric pieces right side up on top, with the two folded edges meeting exactly along the tacking line. Pin and tack in position close to the folded edges.

Topstitch through all three layers an even distance from the centre on each side. The farther apart the two stitching lines, the more the contrasting fabric will show. Remove all the tacking.

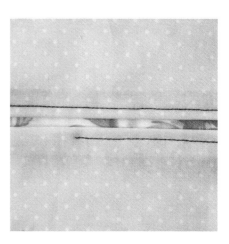

A decorative seam for use with lightweight fabrics.

TOPSTITCHED SEAM

Stitch a plain seam and press it open. Topstitch each side of the seam, taking care to stitch as straight as you can. This is mainly to add decoration, although it does also strengthen the seam and help prevent the raw edges from fraying.

SEAM FINISHES

Even though it is done on the wrong side of the fabric, finishing the raw edges of seams gives the piece a neat and professional look. It also prevents the edges from fraying. For closely woven fabrics, however, a pinked edge is all you need.

Choose matching thread for this, unless your stitching is expertly neat. Our red stitches are for demonstration only!

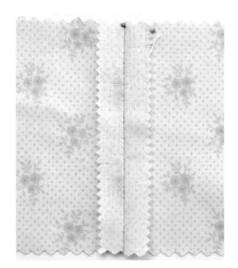

Pinking shears are a quick trick for fabrics that do not fray. When the raw edges are visible, pinking shears also give a decorative finish.

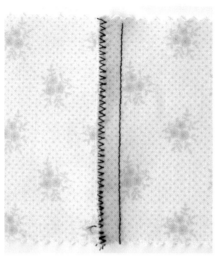

An overlocker can be used if you have one, but this zigzagged edge, created by sewing close to the edge with a zigzag stitch, adds durability.

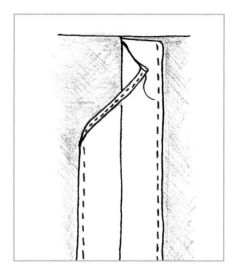

Edges can be turned under and stitched, by folding and pressing the fabric and then stitching either with small neat hand stitches or with the machine.

On sheer fabrics you can make a neat edge by pressing both seam allowances to one side, then rolling both seam allowances together using your thumb and forefinger, and sewing over the edge close to the line of stitching with an even line of hand stitches.

DARTS

Darts create contour. They help turn flat fabric into a three-dimensional shape, and you will use them for almost all garment construction. Darts generally create shape by taking fullness out of the fabric.

Getting the darts right makes a difference as to whether or not the garment fits properly. Whether it's a bust dart, a hip dart or an elbow dart, it is an important construction detail, so take time to make sure it is right. The dart will point to the fullest part of the body – the point of the bust or the curve of the hips. If you take time to sew the dart first with a temporary stitch (basting or tacking), you can make necessary adjustments for a good fit. This will help you avoid common mistakes such as giving yourself pointy boobs or adding inches to your hips with darts that do not flatter.

STANDARD DART
Begin by folding the dart along the marked fold line, with the right sides of the fabric together. Mark the stitching line of the dart with tailor's chalk on the wrong side of the fabric. Pin along the marking and then tack or baste.

Start stitching at the wide part of the dart and stitch along the line carefully,

Darts shape the fabric. This is how a bust dart in a bodice will look.

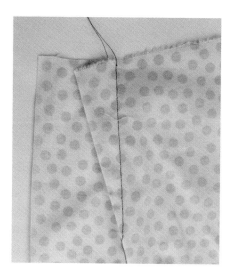

Keep your stitching line straight to create a perfect dart.

From the right side the dart will look like this.

so the dart gradually tapers to nothing. At that point, continue sewing along the fold of the fabric so that the dart does not have a funny pucker at the end. Fasten threads by knotting the ends. Press the dart flat to one side (see overleaf).

DOUBLE-POINTED DART

Fold the fabric with right sides together and mark the stitching line with tailor's chalk on the wrong side of the fabric. Pin and either tack or baste along the marked line. Now stitch, starting at either end, making sure you continue along the fold of the fabric for a few stitches at the beginning and end. Fasten threads by knotting ends. If the dart is wide and will not lie flat, clip up to the line of stitching in the centre of the dart. Press the dart flat to one side.

RELEASED DART

This dart 'releases' fullness at the wider end and is often used to add shaping at the hem or waistline of a garment. With the fabric laid flat, wrong side up, mark the stitching line and a short, straight line at each end of the dart. Fold the fabric with right sides together so that the marked lines match accurately. Pin and then baste or tack along the markings.

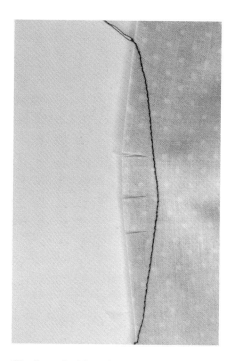

Clipping a double-pointed dart will help the fabric to lie flat.

Start sewing at the point of the dart and be sure to stitch several stitches on the fold before sewing to the full end of the dart. When you reach the top, pivot and sew along the straight marked line to the folded edge. Fasten threads at both ends by tying knots. Press the dart flat to one side.

PRESS DARTS

Pressing the darts you sew, which is done prior to stitching the major seams, really makes a difference. Press on both sides of the dart using the point of the iron along the stitching line, before pressing the dart to one side using a tailor's ham. Place brown paper between the dart and the garment as you press, to prevent ridges.

Vertical darts such as waistline or shoulder darts should be pressed towards the centre front or centre back, while horizontal darts such as bodice darts are pressed downwards.

Deep darts are pressed open with the point pressed flat. If the fabric on a deep dart is thick, you should cut along the fold line of the dart to within about 2 cm (¾ in.) of the point (or even closer if the dart is curved) before pressing it flat.

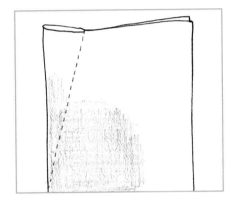

This straight stitched dart is the one you will most often use.

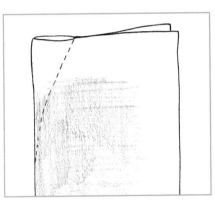

If you are instructed to make a concave dart, it should look like this.

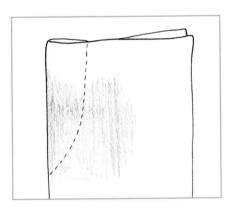

This is what is called a convex dart.

TUCKS

Tucks are slender folds of fabric that are stitched along all or part of their length. They create structure by adding fullness and are also ornamental. The fold is normally formed on the outside of the fabric.

Tucks can be as wide or narrow as you wish. However, if you are adding tucks as a feature without using a pattern, make them before cutting out the fabric, so that you can work out how much fabric you will need. The width of the fabric required will be determined by how far apart you choose to have the tucks. Tucks can be a uniform width apart or can be random widths apart, depending on the look you want.

TYPES OF TUCK

There are three types of tuck, depending on the spacing: blind tucks, in which each tuck overlaps the next; spaced tucks, with a predetermined space between each tuck; and pin tucks, which are very close together. Pin

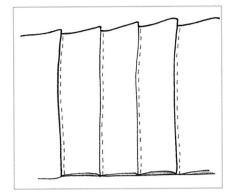

Blind tucks are tucks of fabric that overlap or touch the adjacent ones.

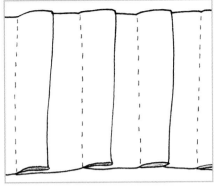

Spaced tucks have gaps between the tucks.

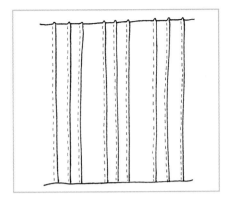

Pin tucks have tiny spaces between them.

tucks are the most popular and are ideal for children's clothes or any fabric that requires delicate decoration.

Decorative tucks, stitched on the right side of the fabric, are usually sewn with matching thread. It looks best if the thread is as close in colour to the fabric as possible.

Pin tucks are often seen on girls' dresses or blouses.

MAKING TUCKS

To mark tucks on fabric, it's best to use a tailor's pencil because tailor's chalk makes too fat a line. You can make a guide by using a piece of card into which you have cut notches indicating the width of a tuck and the space between tucks. This is less fiddly than measuring on the fabric itself.

Fold one tuck along the marked fold line, then lay it flat and press. You need to press each tuck as you stitch it so that every tuck is finished before starting the next. Tucks that have fullness released at one or both ends (known as released tucks) should not have the fullness pressed flat.

Pin and then tack along the length of the tuck to keep it in place as you continue.

Finally, topstitch along the length of the tuck, sewing close to the fold. Remove the tacking.

Pinning is really important. Although it may seem like a step you could miss out, don't!

Try to keep the stitches neat.

PLEATS

Always in style, pleats add a classic design feature to garments and furnishings alike. Pleats are simply folds of fabric that give fullness. Smart-looking permanent pleats are pressed into place. Fabric such as pure cotton will stay crisp and will hold the pleat when pressed. A softer look is achieved by pleating the fabric but leaving it unpressed. Commercially pleated fabric is specially treated, which is why the pleats stay looking tailored for longer.

TYPES OF PLEAT

Knife pleats: fold the edges so they all face in one direction.

Box pleat: for each box pleat, two knife pleats turn towards each other on the wrong side of the fabric so that a box-shaped channel is formed on the right side of the fabric.

Inverted pleats: for each of these, two knife pleats turn towards each other on the right side of the fabric so that a box-shaped channel is formed on the wrong side of the fabric.

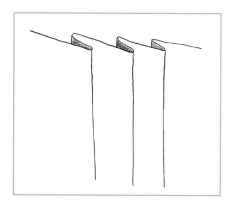

Knife pleats

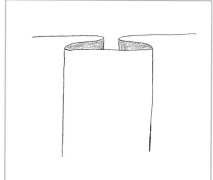

Box pleats

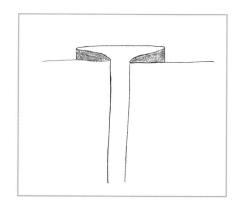

Inverted pleats

MAKING PLEATS

For all types of pleat, transfer the markings indicating the fold lines and stitching or placement lines to the wrong side of the fabric using tailor's chalk and a metre rule (or dressmaker's carbon paper and a tracing wheel if you have them).

Fold each pleat according to the markings. Pin at the top and bottom of each pleat.

Tack the pleat for its entire length, starting at the bottom edge. If you are going to press the pleats, hem the edge of the fabric at this stage.

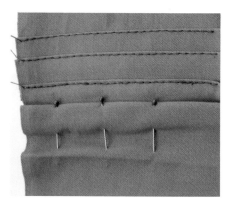

This is the pinning stage of making knife pleats.

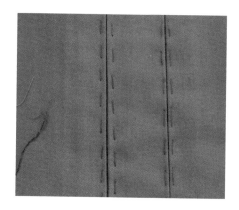

This shows box pleats with tacking stitches holding the pleats in position.

If you are pressing the pleats, place a cloth between the iron and the fabric, and use a steam iron to press along the folds.

If you are stitching them, neatly topstitch close to the folded edge. The stitching can be any length, but because the pleat is there to add fullness, it is usual to stitch the top one tenth of the length of the pleat. However, on a pleated skirt that fits the hip and then flares out, measure from the waistline to where the hip is widest; mark with tailor's chalk, then topstitch along the edge of the pleat from the waistline to the marking. Remove the tacking.

The time spent perfecting your pleats will be well spent. Transferring markings accurately, tacking pleats to keep them in place during preparation, and pressing the pleats properly will all lead to successful results.

FRILLS

A frill is a strip of fabric that is gathered up and attached to a flat piece of fabric – often at the hem, but not always. The fullness of the frill is determined by how long the fabric strip is relative to the main piece. Go for a strip that is twice the length of the main piece if you want it to be fairly full frill, or three times the length for a very full one. A wide frill needs to be really full to look effective.

MAKING A PLAIN FRILL

Hem the lower edge of the frill (and the short ends, if appropriate) with a narrow machine or hand-sewn hem.

Stitch two lines of long gathering stitches, 1 cm (⅜ in.) apart, along the long unhemmed edge of the frill, leaving ends about 8 cm (3 in.) long. Gather the fabric strip until it is the same length as the main fabric piece to which it will be sewn, then wind the thread ends around pins.

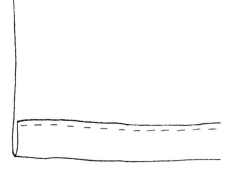

First hem the fabric that will become your frill.

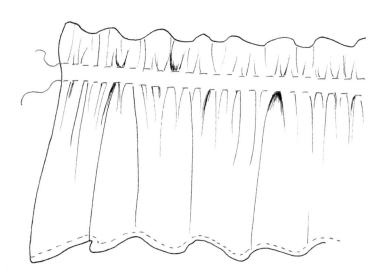

Fiddle with the frill so the gathers are even before you sew it on.

If the fabric strip is particularly long, gather it in sections rather than all at once. Do this by sewing the two rows of gathering stitches for no longer than 20 cm (8 in.), then stop stitching, leave a gap of 1 cm (⅜ in.) and stitch the next 20 cm (8 in.).

This plain frill can be applied in various ways, such as stitching it to extend from an edge; encasing the top edge with bias binding; and stitching it into a seam.

APPLYING A FRILL TO EXTEND FROM AN EDGE
Pin the plain frill to the main piece with right sides together and raw edges even. Adjust the gathers so that they are evenly distributed, and tack or baste in place. Machine stitch the seam. Press the frill away from the main piece and the seam towards the main piece.

A bias strip or ready-made bias binding is used to cover the seam allowances. They are particularly suitable for curved seams.

APPLYING A FRILL USING BIAS BINDING
Pin the plain frill to the main piece with the wrong side of the frill against the right side of the main piece, and raw edges even. Adjust the gathers and tack or baste in place.

With right sides together, pin bias binding (see pp.88–90) to the frill along the raw edge, with the edge of the binding even with the raw edge of the frill. Stitch through all layers (binding, frill and main piece). Wrap the binding over to the wrong side of the main piece, folding the frill away from the fabric, and pin to the fabric. Fold the edge of the bias binding in place and slip stitch it to the main piece.

STITCHING A FRILL INTO A SEAM
Pin the plain frill to the edge of the main piece with right sides together and raw edges even. Adjust the gathers and tack or baste in place.

Place a second fabric piece or a facing on top, right side down and with raw edges even, sandwiching the frill between the two layers. Pin.

Stitch through all three layers, and then turn the facing or second fabric piece to the wrong side, allowing the frill to extend from between the two layers.

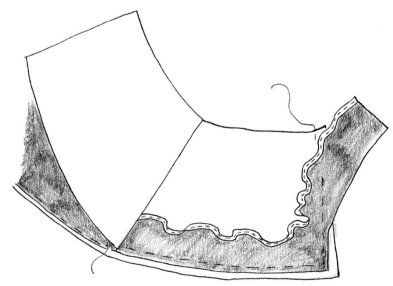

To apply a frill to a faced edge, you must trap the frill between the two layers to sew it in place.

With the facing turned back in position, the frill will 'spill' from the fabric edge.

A frill extending from the edge of a cushion makes a decorative finish.

FRILL WITH A GATHERED TOP

Finish both long edges of the frill (and the short ends, if appropriate) with a narrow machined or hand-sewn hem. Gather the frill as for the plain frill (see pp.41–2) but with the gathering stitches the desired distance down from the top edge.

Pin the frill to the main piece with the wrong side of the frill against the right side of the fabric. Working with the frill on top, baste in place.

Topstitch the frill in place using two rows of stitches 1.5 cm (⅝ in.) apart, centred over the gathering stitches, and then remove the basting and gathering stitches. (See also pp.127–9 for instructions on applying a frill to a blouse or top.)

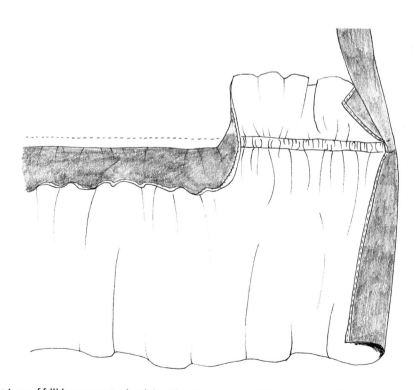

This type of frill is sewn onto the right side of the fabric with the right side of the frill on top.

Frills add an interesting detail to clothing, especially blouses and other tops.

GODETS

Godets are inserts that are used for a decorative effect or to add fullness to the hem of a skirt or sleeve, or even to make trousers flared!

The godet is generally triangular, like a pizza slice. If you are not working from a pattern, you can cut a triangular piece without one, as long as the slash you insert it into is exactly the right length. (You can also insert a godet into a seam by leaving that portion of the seam unstitched.) To calculate the length of the slash, measure from the base of the godet to the pointed end, and then reduce the measurement by the seam allowance.

INSERTING A GODET

Stay stitch (see p.28) along the seam edges of the godet. On the fabric into which it is going to be inserted, stitch up one side and down the other of the marked line where you are going to slash the fabric. To reinforce the top end where the point of the godet will sit, sew a stitch or two back and forth. Cut the fabric from the edge up to the reinforced point. Pin the godet piece to the opening, with right sides together.

Baste or tack along the seam line, matching the seam line to the stay stitching on the godet. The seam allowance will taper to almost nothing

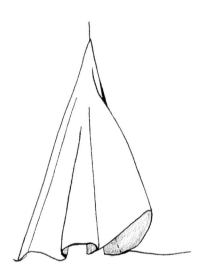

Godets add a decorative flare of fabric to any fabric edge.

at the point of the godet. Machine stitch in place, being careful to take only one stitch across the point at the top of the inset so that the godet remains pointed, rather than having a flat end.

After removing the tacking, press the godet from the wrong side of the fabric.

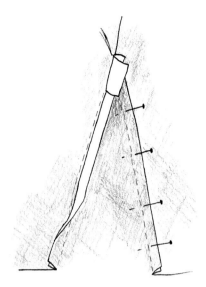

Careful pinning is needed before tacking.

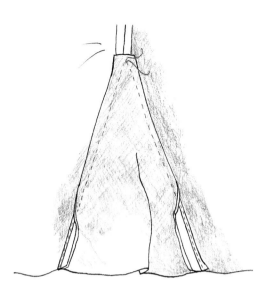

Machine stitch and then take out the tacking.

GATHERS

Gathers are small, soft folds of fabric. They look best when you use fluid fabrics that drape well, but it is possible even to gather bulky fabrics. The secret is to make sure the gathers are evenly dispersed.

Gathering offers a good way of controlling fullness in fabric. It is done by stitching one or two rows of long stitches and drawing them up to form tiny pleats in the fabric. (Shirring is also a type of gathering, in which three or four rows of stitching are used.) You can gather using either hand or machine stitching.

Perfect gathers must be even.

GATHERING USING HAND STITCHING

If you are using hand stitches, make them small and evenly spaced. Start off with a few back stitches, and then use a running stitch, leaving ends about 8 cm (3 in.) long. Pull gently on the thread at one end of the row of stitching until the section measures the length you want. Wrap the thread ends around pins, and distribute the gathers evenly.

GATHERING USING MACHINE STITCHING

To gather using a sewing machine, set the dial to the longest stitch length. Sew a row or two of straight stitching in the required place. Take the fabric away from the sewing machine before pulling gently on the thread(s) and gathering up the fabric along the line(s) of stitching. Even out the gathers and wrap the thread ends around pins to secure.

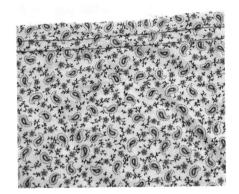

One or two rows of long stitches are used to make the gathering.

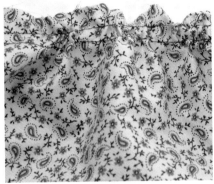

Pull gently on one row of stitches and the fabric will gather up. You will need to distribute the gathers to get them even.

TIP　IF YOU ARE GATHERING A LARGE AREA, SUCH AS THE WAIST OF A FULL GATHERED SKIRT, DIVIDE THE AREA TO BE GATHERED INTO SECTIONS – SAY, FOUR. SEW YOUR LONG STITCHES ALONG THE FIRST SECTION, THEN STOP SEWING, LEAVING THREAD ENDS THAT YOU CAN GET HOLD OF, TO GATHER THE FABRIC UP LATER. START THE SECOND SECTION VERY CLOSE TO THE FIRST AND CONTINUE UNTIL YOU HAVE SEWN THE WHOLE AREA. THIS IS HELPFUL AS THE THREAD IS LESS LIKELY TO BREAK.

PRESSING GATHERS

With the gathered fabric wrong side up, use the iron to press the fabric. Work from the smooth part of the fabric up into the gathers, so that the point of the iron goes touches the row of stitches. Do not press the hot iron onto the line of gathering as this will spoil the fullness, and the look, of the gathered fabric.

Gathered or pleated fabric added to the bottom of a skirt or dress is known as a flounce.

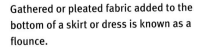

Gathering adds fullness and also softens the line of the fabric. It is seen on a lot of children's clothing.

This little girl's dress has gathering at the armhole (gathered trim at shoulder) and at the waist (gathered skirt)

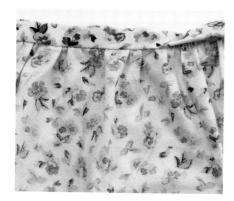

To make a simple gathered skirt, first cut your fabric to create a piece that, ungathered, is wide enough to fit your hips comfortably. Gather it up until it equals your waist measurement plus 5 cm (2 in.) to allow for a fastening at the gathered edge. The length of the skirt is up to you. Add a waistband (see pp.112–13).

Lightly press the gathered top of the skirt before sewing the one seam required – it's usual to place this at the back. Add a fastening, such as a zip, hem your skirt, and wear it – or put it on the little miss you've made it for!

FACINGS

Facings are pieces of fabric that are usually cut separately and applied to a section of a garment, to give a neat finish to a raw edge. Facings support the shape and finish the edge of necklines, armholes and collars.

A facing always needs to be cut on the same grain as the piece you are attaching it to, so be aware of this and cut the facing on the lengthwise grain if the fabric is cut on the lengthwise grain. The facing piece needs to 'fit' the fabric piece, which will be easy enough if you are using a pattern – just remember to cut with accuracy. If you are making your own facing, you will need to trace the shape of the edge you wish to face using tracing paper to create a pattern piece that is at least 6 cm (2¼ in.) in depth. Cut the facing from fabric using the paper pattern.

There are many differently shaped facing pieces. Some are actually cut as one piece with the garment piece and are, in effect, 'folded back'. Others are used to face more than one edge – for example, a single facing that edges the neckline and armhole piece. These require a careful ordering of instructions, which has been covered in the 'Easy Steps to Making ...' section of chapter 9, Get Sewing! Most facings are applied as per the instructions given here.

APPLYING A SIMPLE FACING

It is advisable to stay stitch around the edge to be faced. If the facing is made up of more than one piece, join the pieces together.

If the fabric is sheer and lightweight, edge the facing by turning under a narrow hem, but do not do this if the fabric is bulky. Use pinking shears if the fabric does not fray easily. For a fancy finish, add bias binding to the edge of the facing.

Hem the facing piece if the fabric is not bulky. This is an armhole facing.

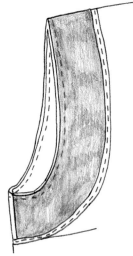

The facing is pinned, tacked and then stitched, with right sides together, to the fabric edge it will face.

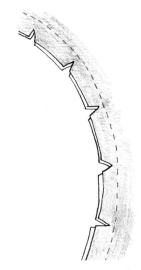

Carefully clip up to, but not through, the stitching to help the facing lie flat.

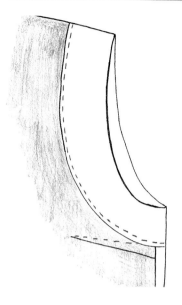

Place the facing and the main fabric piece with right sides together and raw edges even. Stitch a plain seam.

Clip notches in any curved edges so the fabric will be smooth.

Turn the facing to the inside. Press, using a cloth between the iron and the fabric.

A facing produces a tidy finish on the inside and outside of the garment or edge. This shows the facing on the inside of the garment.

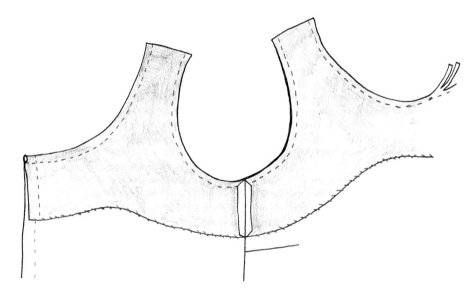

You will often find that a commercial pattern gives you an all-in-one arm-and-neck facing. Use a slip stitch to hold the bottom edge of the facing down at its hem.

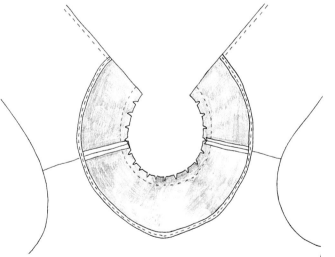

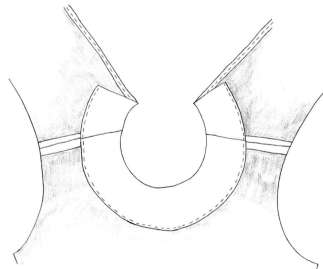

A neck facing will look like this at the stage when it is hemmed, applied, and clipped to ease the curve.

This is how the neck facing will look when it is turned to the inside of the garment. Always press the facings without using much pressure to avoid creating a ridge at the edge.

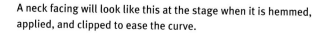

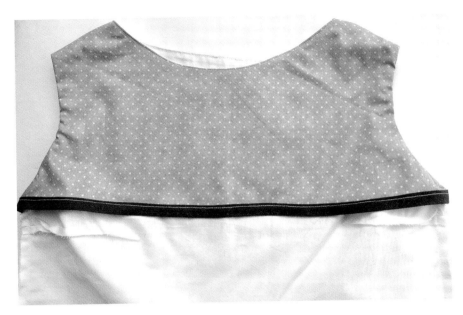

Bias binding can be used to edge a facing.

Binding is an alternative finish to a facing.

CREATING A NEAT EDGE USING BIAS BINDING

Using a bias binding (see pp.88–9) in a contrasting fabric creates an interesting design feature.

Stay stitch around the edge you will be facing, and then pin the binding around the edge, with right sides together and raw edges even. You will need to ease the binding onto it, especially around corners. Tack and then stitch a seam close to the edge.

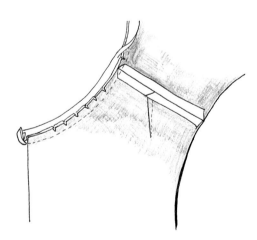

With right sides together, pin, tack and stitch the binding to the edge you are facing.

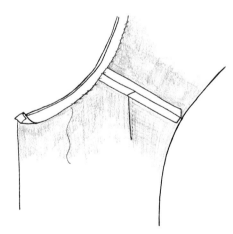

Hand sew the binding to the wrong side of the fabric to finish.

Wrap the binding over the edge to the wrong side of the fabric. Pin in place, turning under the edges as you do so. Slip stitch the turned-under edge of the binding to the fabric.

FACING AN OUTWARD CORNER

Cut a strip of fabric on the straight grain. Pin this facing to the fabric with right sides together. At the corner, fold the facing to form a crease with the grain lines at right angles. Continue pinning the facing piece to the garment as far as you need to.

Stitch a diagonal seam at the corner point along the diagonal fold. Trim 1 cm (⅜ in.) from the seam allowance and press this mitred seam open. Stitch the facing to the fabric with a straight seam, pivoting at the corner.

Turn the facing to the wrong side of the fabric you are facing, and pin in place, turning under the edges of the facing as you do so. Slip stitch the facing to the fabric.

FACING AN INWARD CORNER

Cut a strip of fabric on the straight grain. Pin this facing to the garment with right sides together. At the corner fold the facing in a diagonal crease from the point, and then fold a straight crease even with the edge of the facing.

Stitch the facings together along the diagonal crease marking.

Trim 1 cm (⅜ in.) from the seam allowance and press open. Continue pinning before stitching with a straight seam, pivoting at the corner.

Turn the facing to the wrong side of the fabric you are facing, and pin in place, turning under the edges of facing as you do so. Slip stitch the facing to the fabric.

INTERFACINGS

Interfacings are used to add body to details such as collars or cuffs, and in tailoring to stiffen garments such as a bodice. It comes in both fusible and non-fusible versions. Usually the fabric is especially made for the purpose of interlining, and is an inexpensive white fabric, but in fact you can interface with any fabric as long as it is not bulky.

TIP   FACINGS PROVIDE A NEAT FINISH BUT IT IS ESSENTIAL THAT THEY ARE PRESSED WITH CARE. ROLL THE SEAM BETWEEN FINGER AND THUMB SO THAT IT IS NOT VISIBLE — IT SHOULD BE SLIGHTLY UNDER THE FRONT EDGE OF THE GARMENT. ALWAYS PRESS USING A CLOTH BETWEEN THE IRON AND THE FABRIC.

LININGS AND UNDERLININGS

Underlinings and linings add another layer to the garment or item you are making. Fabric for underlinings and also linings must have the same durability qualities as the fashion fabric – both must be able to be washed in the same way, must shrink the same amount and must be able to be ironed at the same temperature. (Do not choose, for example, a lining that has to be dry cleaned if your fabric is washable!) The difference between underlinings and linings is in the construction.

Underlining

The main use for an underlining in a garment is to help keep the shape of the garment. Often the use of an underlining improves the look of the fabric, because with an underlining in place the fabric creases less. In the case of garments, both linings and underlinings provide a layer between the wearer and the main fabric, and this is often flattering for the wearer – for example, a skirt will cling less to the wearer's lumps and bumps if it is lined. Underlinings are less likely to be used around armholes or cuffs as they provide too much bulk.

Underlinings and fashion fabrics are sewn together to act as one layer. Cut the underlining pieces using the same pattern pieces as the garment pieces, with all the same construction markings and on the same grain line. Cut them so that the right side of the underlining fabric will show on the inside of the garment.

Pin the underlining and fabric together, matching any notches and seam lines. Now baste the two pieces – fabric and underlining – together. From that point on, treat the underlining and the fabric as one fabric, until the hemming stage.

Hem by turning the garment hem allowance over the underlining and attach it to the underlining only.

Lining

Lining preserves shape, reduces wrinkling, adds body to soft fabric and makes the inside of your garment look as good as the outside! It is cut and assembled separately from the fabric and is then sewn into the garment or item by hand or machine.

Lining gives a neat finish, as the garment is lined in one piece rather than sections, with no seams on show at all. This is achieved by cutting the same pieces from lining fabric as fabric, and constructing the fabric and the lining as two separate garments, which sit one inside the other when construction is complete.

To line an entire dress, see pp.109–11. In the case of skirts and trousers, instructions for sewing the garment are to be followed when making the lining. The lining is then placed inside the garment, with the wrong sides of the fabric together. Construction markings must be matched for accuracy, and the garment and lining should be basted together at the waist before the waistband is attached. When the garments are turned in the right way, the right side of the lining will be on the inside of the garment.

Finishing touches are best done by hand. Slip stitch the lining to the placket of the fastening, and hem the lining separately, slightly shorter than the fabric at the edge of the skirt or trousers.

The most important thing to remember when you are planning to line a garment or item is that the accuracy in size and shape of the lining pieces is of paramount importance. Wrongly cut pieces will distort the look of the finished garment.

HEMS

Hems matter, especially on garments. Making sure they are not bulky and are pressed carefully to prevent ridges is important. Stitch evenly if you want a hem that gets noticed for the right reasons.

MARK IT

Whether you are hemming curtains or a skirt, let them hang overnight before hemming so that the fabric will drop with its own weight, to where it wants to be!

Get help if you are hemming a garment. It needs to be on a model when the hem is marked. Using pins is the quickest way to mark a hem; make sure they are thin dressmaker's pins that will not leave noticeable holes. Start at the front, making a decision as to how much fabric you need to turn up. Using a long ruler as a guide, place pins on the fabric to mark where the hem will be – say, every 5 cm (2 in.). Do not turn the fabric up for this – concentrate on marking out the hemline as accurately as possible.

PREPARE IT

Lay out the marked item on a flat surface and turn up the hem to meet the pin markings exactly. Tack the hem in place 2.5 cm (1 in.) from the folded edge, removing the pins as you go. Press lightly, placing spare fabric between the iron and your garment or item.

Trim the edge of the turned-up fabric so that the hem allowance is the same width along its length. If the edge is fuller then the fabric at the point where it is to be sewn, distribute the fullness by hand sewing a long running stitch and gently gathering the fabric along the thread, as you would when making gathers.

PREPARE THE EDGE

Finish the edge of the hem in one of the following ways, depending on the fabric.

- If the fabric does not fray, you could neaten the edge with pinking shears.
- For most fabrics you could use a zigzag stitch, which needs to be right at the edge of the fabric to give it a good finish.
- If the fabric is not bulky, you could turn under the edge with a machine stitch with a tiny seam allowance.
- For something very special – such as suiting, lightweight or sheer fabrics – you could bind the edge with a narrow bias binding.

When the edge is finished you are ready to sew the hem using either hand stitches or the sewing machine.

A zigzag stitch stops the edge from fraying.

HAND-STITCHED HEMS

Here are two hand stitches commonly used for hems. (See also p.15.)

Slip stitch: This is great if the fabric is lightweight or sheer. Make a stitch in the hem fabric about 3 mm (⅛ in.) long. Take the needle through to the under fabric, which is what will show from the right side, and here pick up only two or three threads so that the stitch will be barely visible from the right side. Continue taking a stitch through the fold and then a few threads in the under fabric, along the hemline. Finish with a knot close to the fabric, on the wrong side.

Hemming stitch: This is fine for any fabric. The stitch looks like a diagonal row of stitches on the inside but on the outside it doesn't show at all – or shouldn't! Bringing the needle through from the back of the work, take only one thread of the fabric from the right side, then bring the needle through the fold of the hem edge. Continue to work the needle at a backwards slant to create stitches that slant forwards. It's crucial that you pick up only one thread from the front for the stitches not to show on the right side.

MACHINE-STITCHED HEMS

For this, the edge only has to be finished with pinking, zigzag stitching or a turned edge. Then simply turn the edge under 3 mm (⅛ in.) and stitch close to the edge as neatly as you can.

With lightweight fabric it is enough to turn the fabric just once to make a tiny hem, which is then machine stitched.

HAND-ROLLED HEMS

This involves using the sewing machine and hand stitches, to create a hem that is a bit special. It is suitable for sheer fabrics and silks, and for use on items such as scarves and sashes.

Machine stitch a row of stitches 3 mm (⅛ in.) from the fabric edge.

Trim close to the fabric.

Roll the fabric between the thumb and forefinger of your left hand, pinning the hem in place as you go.

Use a slip stitch to hem the 'roll' in position.

FASTENINGS

PLACKETS

A placket can be used to finish off an opening in a seam. It is usually faced or hemmed to look neat. The placket itself is a fabric strip that laps around both sides of a slash in the fabric or an opening.

Garment patterns will include pattern pieces for plackets as required. However, if you wish to make a placket for an opening in a seam and do not have a pattern piece, cut a facing piece which is twice the length of the opening in the seam.

With right sides together, pin, tack and sew the facing to the opening, with the edges of the facing and the opening even. As you sew, you will need to open out the opening in the seam as flat as possible. Stitch down one side, pivot at the end of the opening and stitch up to the top of the opening.

Turn the free edge of the facing to the wrong side of the fabric and press into place. Hem the placket onto the seam line to complete.

To make a faced placket that finishes a slash in the fabric, rather than in a seam, cut a facing 10 cm (4 in.) wide and 1 cm (⅜ in.) longer than the opening will be. Turn the long edges under and press. Pin the facing to the area that you are going to slash for the opening. In the centre of the facing, use tailor's chalk to mark a line as long you want the opening to be.

Stitch through all layers with a straight stitch, both sides of the marked line, starting 1 cm (⅜ in.) from the edge, and tapering to a point. Take one extra stitch across the point at the top. Slash through the fabric, between the stitching, to the point.

Turn the facing to the inside of the newly made opening and press. Tack and hem the turned-in edges over the seam. Stitch the upper edges together.

Often plackets may be fastened with a zip or buttonholes. Alternatively, poppers or hooks-and-eyes can be sewn on for a quick fix. By contrast, if you want a special finish, rouleau loops are the ultimate fastening. Fastenings are often left until last when sewing. This can sometimes mean that they do not get the same amount of attention as other areas of construction, but, for a smart finish, it is worth spending time making the fastening look fantastic.

ZIPS

These can be inserted by either hand or machine. If you use a machine, it is essential to use a proper zipper foot. Most sewing machines are provided with one, though each machine has slightly different feet. The zipper foot you use must be one that is made for your particular machine, and must also suit the type of zip that you are putting in. Match the thread to your fabric. The instructions given here are for centred zips (ideal for a central position, such as down the back of a dress), lapped zips (useful for zips in side seams) and concealed zips (invisible, apart from the pull). A seam allowance of 2.5 cm (1 in.) should be used whichever method you are using to insert your zip.

Putting in a centred zip by hand

This method is for the edge-to-edge insertion of a zip, with it placed centrally, and the teeth in line with the seam. Using hand stitching is a good method for the inexperienced machinist but is also great for a professional look. Bespoke items almost always have zips inserted by hand. The good thing is that, by using tiny hand stitches, the process is very controllable, and you are not going to need several attempts to get it right.

The seam is sewn before you begin to insert the zip. Mark the length of the zip on the wrong side of the fabric with a tailor's chalk dot on the seam allowance. Neaten the edges of the seam with pinking shears or a zigzag stitch. Machine baste the seam for the length of the zip, and use a normal stitch length for the remainder of the seam. Press the seam open.

Lay the fabric on a flat surface wrong side up. Place the zip face down on the basted seam, with the teeth centred over the seam line. Pin and tack the zipper tape to the fabric along both sides of the teeth, working through all layers and making sure that the teeth of the zip stay over the seam.

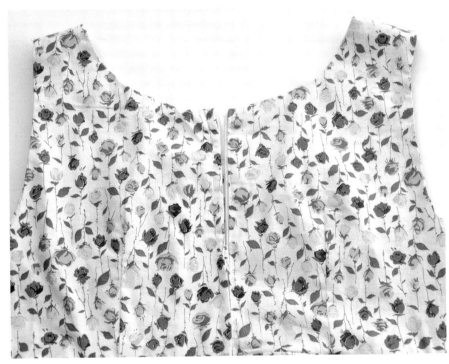

Sew the zip in place using a prick stitch. This is a tiny stitch, evenly spaced, which takes only a thread or two from the front and then makes another tiny stitch on the inside of the fabric – in this case, on the zip, as it is sewn close to the zip teeth. Some seamstresses prefer to sew from the right side, so that they can be sure that the prick stitch is unnoticeable.

Remove the tacking stitches and unpick the basted part of the seam (using an unpicker if you have one) to reveal the teeth of the zip.

Hand stitching a zip gives more accuracy because it is easy to control – just make sure your stitches are neat.

Putting in a centred zip by machine

This is the machined-stitched edge-to-edge method of inserting a zip, with the zip placed centrally, and the teeth in line with the seam.

The seam is sewn before you begin to insert the zip with this method. Mark the length of the zip on the wrong side of the fabric with a tailor's chalk dot on the seam allowance. Neaten the edges of the seam with pinking shears or a zigzag stitch. Machine baste the seam for the length of the zip, and use a normal stitch length for the remainder of the seam. Press the seam open.

Lay the fabric on a flat surface wrong side up. Place the zip face down on the basted seam, with the teeth centred over the seam.

Pin and tack the zipper tape to the fabric along both sides of the teeth, working through all layers and making sure that the teeth of the zip stay over the seam.

Turn the work over on the flat surface so it is right side up. Using a tailor's pencil, mark a stitching line surrounding the zip on the right side. With the zipper foot on the opposite side of the needle to the teeth, start stitching at the bottom of the zip, and stitch along the marked line. Stop before the zip pull. Keep the needle in as you lift the presser foot. Undo the zip to where you have stitched already. With the zip pull out of the way behind the presser foot, place the presser foot down again and continue sewing to the top of the zip. Remove from the machine.

Put the zipper foot on the other side of the needle. Insert the needle where you started stitching at the bottom of the first side, making sure it is below the teeth of the zip. Stitch across the base and when you get to the other stitching line, pivot the fabric and continue stitching up that side. At the top, deal with the zip pull in the same way as before.

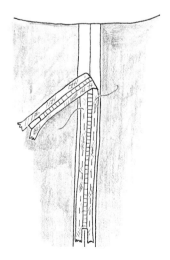

Before the zip is machine stitched, it is tacked in place with the teeth over the seam line.

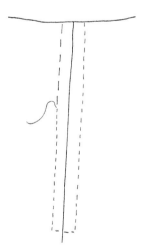

After it has been tacked, the zip is machine stitched in place from the right side of the fabric.

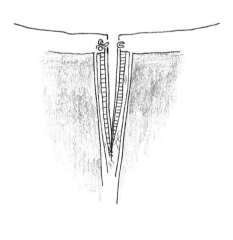

Finish the fastening by sewing a hook and eye at the top of the zip (see p.63).

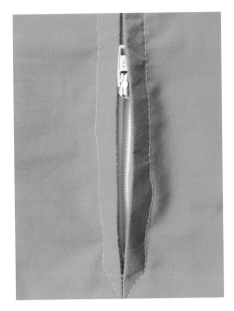

Centred zips that sit behind the zip look neat and are fairly easy to do.

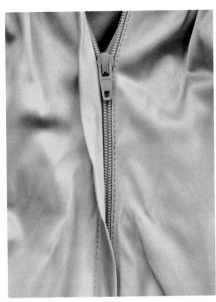

Choose a zip that matches the colour of your fabric.

Remove the tacking stitches and unpick the basted part of the seam (using an unpicker if you have one) to reveal the teeth of the zip.

Putting in a lapped zip by machine

This zip is covered by a narrow, one-sided flap.

Before you begin to insert the zip, prepare the opening. Mark the length of the zip on the wrong side of the seam with tailor's chalk. Stitch the seam but leave an opening the length of the zip. Press back the seam allowance on both sides.

For this type of zip, the lap is on the left side of the garment, to cover the zip (which should be inserted into the left-hand side seam). Position the zip so that the right-hand edge of the zip teeth lines up with the seam line, thereby extending the left-hand seam allowance.

Place the zip behind the fold of the right-hand seam allowance and pin in position. Tack to hold in place and remove the pins.

With the needle position to far left on the zipper foot, and starting at the bottom of the zip, machine stitch the zip to the right-hand seam allowance along the marked line, sewing as close to the zip teeth as possible. Stop before the zip pull. Keep the needle in as you lift the presser foot, and then undo the zip to where you have stitched already. With the zip pull out of the way, behind the presser foot, place the presser foot down again and continue sewing to the top of the zip.

Turn the fabric to the right side and press, avoiding the zip pull.

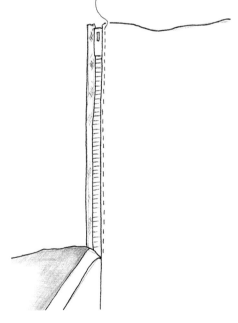

Secure the right-hand side of the zip in position behind the pressed-back seam allowance.

Tack through all layers to attach the unstitched side of the zip to the fabric, starting at the bottom of the zip.

Sew two rows of tacking – one must keep the lap in the position you want it to be, covering the zip, and the other must go through two layers of fabric and secure the zip tape on the left-hand side.

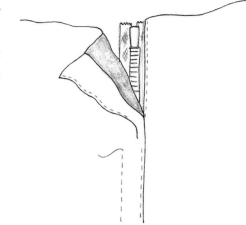

To form the 'lap' of the zip, continue to sew with the needle in the far left position. Start by sewing across the base of the zip before pivoting and sewing 1 cm (⅜ in.) from the seam line just to the side of the tacking stitch to avoid getting tangled. Lift the presser foot up, in order to pull the zip pull behind the line of stitching, as before. Backstitch at the top to anchor stitching.

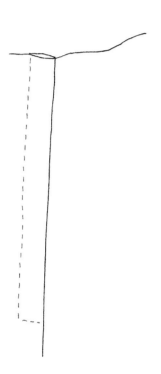

The final stitching will secure the zip in place and will also form topstitching that outlines the lap.

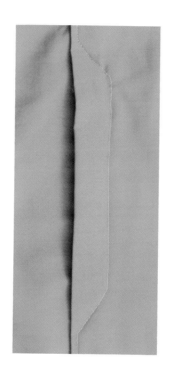
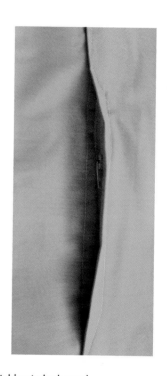

The lapped method requires straight stitching to look good.

Putting in a concealed zip by machine

This is the easiest of all zip methods, but it is essential that you use the special machine foot, which has grooves underneath it, through which the teeth of the zip slide. For this method you do not sew the seam until after the zip has been inserted into it.

Neaten the edges of the seam with pinking shears or a zigzag machine stitch. Fold the seam allowance to the wrong side along the seam line and press along the crease line.

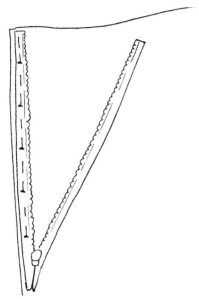

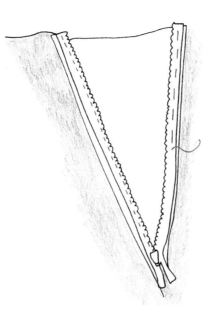

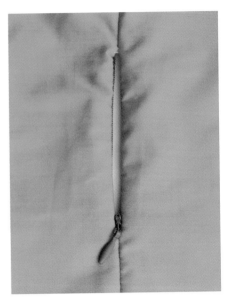

Pin, tack, then sew the first side of the zip in place.

Uncurl the zip feet as you stitch.

Concealed zips are easy to insert.

Open out the seam allowance with the fabric right side up. Place the open zip face down on the seam allowance with the zip teeth lined up on the crease. Pin in place.

Using the invisible zip foot, stitch the zip to the crease line. The zip teeth need to be in the groove under the zip foot. As you stitch, gently uncurl the zip teeth. Sew as far as you can go towards the bottom of the zip.

Repeat for the other side of the zip, this time stitching it to the other seam allowance, from top to bottom. Make sure the zip teeth are in line with the crease line.

Change to a normal foot. Pin the remainder of the seam together and stitch to close the seam, starting where the zip stitching ends. Backstitch at the start of this seam, to strengthen the area at the base of the zip.

BUTTONHOLES

Buttons are an important finishing touch as well as having a practical purpose, but making buttonholes is a job many beginners dread, as they need practice. Have a go on spare fabric, until you are happy with the results. Instructions for sewing on buttons are given on pp.17–18.

Check to see how the buttons will look before you begin to work on the buttonholes, and plan where you want them to go. Here are a few guidelines on placement:

- Buttonholes are usually placed at least 1 cm (⅜ in.) from the edge.

- The top buttonhole on a garment is placed at least half the width of the button from the neckline edge.
- The last button on a dress should be around 10 cm (4 in.) from the hem edge.
- If your buttons are big, you may want to use fewer buttons and space them out, whereas little buttons need to be placed close together.

Buttonholes can be horizontal or vertical. Vertical buttonholes hold buttons less securely. It is a good idea to interface any fabric that will have buttonholes, to strengthen it.

There are a variety of ways to make a buttonhole, and most of these use a sewing machine. Today's sewing machines usually have an automatic buttonhole setting, but it is still possible to make neat buttonholes if yours doesn't.

Machine-worked buttonholes
Mark the position of the buttonholes with tailor's chalk.

Choose the button first so that you know how long a buttonhole to make. Make the buttonhole longer than the width of the button by 2 mm (just under ⅛ in.), but not any longer than that. Machine baste the line where the slash will be made.

Using a close-together zigzag stitch, sew along the length of the mark. At the end, pivot and then sew with a slightly longer stitch for one or two securing stitches.

Pivot again, and sew in the other direction with a close-together zigzag stitch back along the other side of the marked line. The two rows of stitching should be 1 mm (less than ¹/₁₆ in.) apart but should not touch.

At the end of the second row of stitching, pivot again, and sew with a slightly longer stitch for one or two stitches to complete the buttonhole.

Use a buttonholing tool, or a sharp blade, to cut through the fabric on the basting line between the two rows of zigzag stitching.

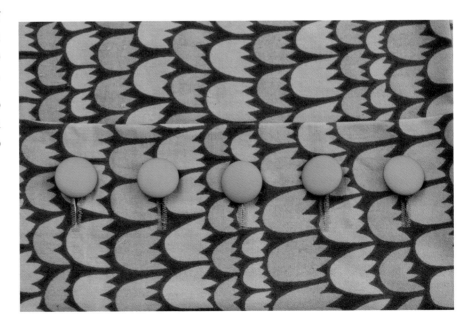

Machine-worked buttonholes look smart and the over-sized buttons add a feature to this cushion cover.

Hand-worked buttonholes

Mark the position of the buttonholes with tailor's chalk.

Machine baste or tack on the line where the slash will be made (see advice on buttonhole length on previous page). Cut along this line.

Work along the marked line with tiny blanket stitches, otherwise known as buttonhole stitch, sewing from left to right and overstitching with long straight stitches at each end.

Bound buttonholes

These are for special occasions only! They take a while to master and are a bit fiddly, but give a really high-quality finish. There are various methods but this one works well.

First make a tailor's chalk mark on the fabric where you will make the buttonhole.

For the piece to 'bind' the buttonhole, cut a strip of fabric on the lengthwise grain, making it 2.5 cm (1 in.) wide and 2.5 cm (1 in.) longer than the finished buttonhole. Make a lengthwise mark down the centre of the strip. Fold in the edges so that they meet at the centre marking; press.

With right sides together place the folded fabric strip on the buttonhole marking, with the centre running along the buttonhole marking. Pin in place.

Stitching through the fabric strip and the garment or item, sew around the buttonhole, stitching down both sides and across both ends 5 mm (¼ in.) from the centre, pivoting at the corners.

Cut along the centre marking and then cut diagonally into the corners. Turn the strip to the wrong side through the opening. The folded edges will form bindings that should meet at the centre.

On the right side of the fabric, fold the main fabric over the buttonhole to reveal triangular ends. Stitch these to the ends of the binding to form corners.

Hand sew the bound buttonhole on the wrong side to keep it together, and press using a cloth between the iron and the fabric.

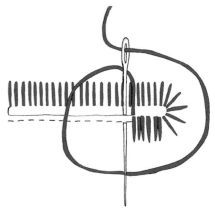

Sewing buttonhole stitch around the slash will stop it from fraying and form the hand-worked buttonhole.

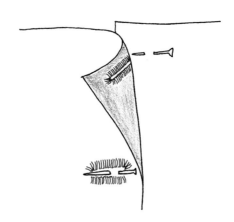

Mark with a pin where the button should go.

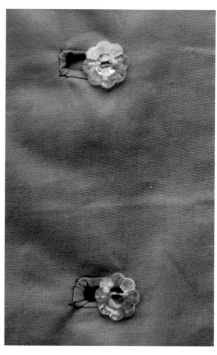

These are bound buttonholes using self-fabric and matching buttons.

OTHER FASTENINGS

Press studs

These are efficient at holding fabrics together, giving a flat closure that is not visible from the right side of the fabric, and they come in various sizes. The bigger ones are fine for heavier fabrics, but as a general rule, press studs are best for lightweight fabrics, where there is little strain.

The ball part of the press stud is sewn on to the underside of the overlap of the fabric and the socket part is sewn to the top of the underlap. Mark the position for the ball part on the overlap first. Secure in position by sewing overhand stitches through each hole, taking the thread under the press stud from one hole to the next. Catch only a few threads on the right side of the fabric so that the stitches do not show.

When the ball part is secured, close the opening of the fabric and, pushing a pin through the centre hole of the ball section, mark the position for the socket section. Attach the socket section in the same way as the ball section.

Press studs need lots of stitches to keep them safely in place.

Hooks and eyes

Available in different sizes, hooks and eyes can be used on all fabric weights. Often they are used above a zip, and they are also used on their own as a secure fastener.

Where you have overlapping fabric, use a straight 'bar' type of eye. Sew the hook to the underside of the overlap and sew the eye to the top of the underlap. Make sure they are in line with each other. Each part should be sewn with tiny overhand stitches that hardly show through on the right side of the fabric.

Where you have edges that meet, use a curved eye. Sew the hook to one side and the eye to the other, positioning the eye so that it extends beyond the edge. Make sure the hook and eye are in line with each other.

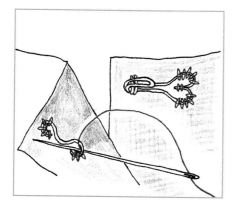

On overlapping edges, the hook is sewn to the overlap and the eye to the underlap.

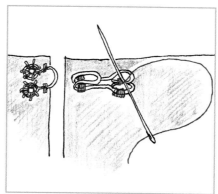

If edges meet, use a hook and eye in which the eye is curved.

Heavy, flat metal hooks are used for trousers as they are more durable.

Thread loops

A thread loop is made from thread – embroidery silks are ideal – and used with a button as delicate detail that is also perfectly practical. Thread the needle with a double thread and make a loop on the right side of a garment using small backstitches at each end of the loop. Sew several of these loops on top of each other, securing each with backstitches, and then 'wrap' the thread around the loops using a close blanket stitch (see p.14), to make one thread loop. Lap the closing to sew the button under the thread loop.

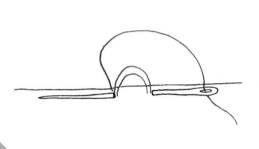

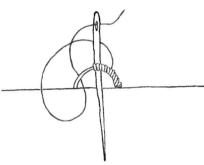

First create some loops of thread on the right side of the garment.

Now make the thread loop thicker by sewing over and over the thread with blanket stitch.

These delicate thread loops look really pretty.

Rouleau loops

Though time-consuming to make, the button loops known as rouleau loops add an impressive touch to any item. They are made from bias strips stitched into narrow tubes and are inserted into a seam.

Cut the bias strips to twice the desired width, plus 1 cm (⅜ in.), and join the ends to form one long strip (see p.89). Fold the strip in half lengthwise, with right sides together. Pin and stitch a 5 mm (¼ in.) seam, leaving the ends open. Do not trim the seam allowance – as this bulks up the rouleau. Turn the rouleau right side out – you may need a blunt needle to do this. Do not press.

Cut the long rouleau into individual rouleau loops, each long enough to fit over the chosen button, plus two seam allowances. Be sure to cut them all to exactly the same length.

Pin the loops, evenly spaced, to the right side of the fabric edge that you are closing, with the loops facing

Use bias strips to make rouleau loops.

inwards. Pin and stitch a facing to the right side of the edge, with the facing turning inwards. Fold the facing to the wrong side of the fabric, so that the loops now face outwards.

Sew buttons in position to match the loops, on the other side of the fabric you wish to close. Buttons covered with matching fabric make a really fancy finish with these rouleau loops.

Rouleau loops give a special finish, which is worth the effort as they look great on bridal or evening wear.

This bag is decorated with loads of rouleau loops. It was made by Donna Angelina who is in her eighties and is a friend from Portugal.

Ribbon can be threaded through these metal rings to lace up a bodice or provide decoration. However, they need a special little tool to apply them to the fabric. Eyelets, shown here, can also be used as a fastening.

6 Design details

THE SHAPE OF THE SLEEVE, THE TYPE OF COLLAR, and the choice of cuff, are design details that make your garment individual. You will mostly be working from a commercial pattern that you have chosen specifically because you like its design features, but as you gain experience you may like to adapt the details by altering the shape of the pattern pieces. For minor changes this is not too complicated; for example, if you are changing the length or shape of a sleeve, you need only be careful to keep the shape of the armhole and the sleeve cap the same as they appear on the pattern to ensure the fit is accurate. Some instructions for alterations will come with the pattern, but here are some tried and tested methods that may make things that little bit easier, or may make the addition of a cuff or a collar – where there isn't one on the pattern – a possibility!

POCKETS

Pockets set the style of a garment. Even if you are inexperienced at sewing, take time to work on the pockets, as they become a noticeable feature of your creation.

Position the pockets where your hands would naturally slip into them, unless they are purely a decorative feature. All pockets are meant to be functional but most are decorative as well. Use the same fabric as for the main piece, unless you are deliberately going for contrast – say, a plain pocket on a patterned piece, or vice versa. If you have patterned fabric and are adding a patch of the same patterned fabric, cut the patch from a piece that matches up with the pattern perfectly.

There are lots of variations of pocket, but they fall into two main types. One type is applied on top of the garment – a patch pocket is an example of this type. The other type is pushed to the inside of a seam or slash and is made usually from lining fabric. This type sometimes has a flap or welt concealing the opening.

PATCH POCKETS

These are sewn to the outside of the fabric. Usually the patch is rectangular or square, with square or rounded corners. The pockets can be lined or not, and can have a flap as an extra feature.

The first job is to mark the position of the patch pocket with tailor's tacks, stitches or a basting stitch on the right side of the fabric.

Unlined patch pockets

Turn under and machine stitch a narrow hem on the top edge of the patch. Fold the top edge to the right side, creating a self-facing, and machine stitch the two layers together at the sides. Snip off the corners of the seam allowance at the top, and turn right side out.

If the lower edge is curved, stitch with a basting stitch around the curves just inside the seam line, pulling the threads so the rounded corners will turn in. Also clip into the curves within the seam allowance. This stitch is used to keep fabric in place, for ease of sewing, and is sometimes referred to as an ease stitch. On patches with square corners, snip off the corners within the seam allowance to reduce bulk. Turn under the seam allowances on the remaining edges, and tack. Slip stitch the self-facing in place, making sure the stitches aren't noticeable on the right side.

Press the pocket and pin and tack in place, right side up, on the right side of the fabric. Topstitch around the sides and bottom of the pocket close to the edge, using matching or contrasting thread, or, if you don't want to see the stitching, use a tiny slip stitch with matching thread. Remove the tacking.

Lined patch pockets

Cut the lining so it is the same shape as the pocket but only three quarters of the length. With right sides together and the top raw edges even, pin and stitch the lining to the pocket at the upper edge, leaving a 2.5 cm (1 in.) opening in the centre of the seam; press.

Fold the pocket so that the remaining edges of the pocket and lining are even, which means that the stitched seam is no longer at the top. Stitch close to the remaining raw edges, trim the seam allowance and turn the pocket right side out through the gap in the top seam. Slip stitch the seam closed. Press, using a cloth between the flap and the iron. Attach the lined patch pocket to the right side of the fabric, as for the unlined patch pocket (above).

Lined flap for a patch pockets

Cut out the flap and lining so they are the same size (and as wide as the pocket). Pin the lining to the flap with right sides together and stitch along the side and bottom edges. Turn right side out. If desired, topstitch around the edge to match the topstitching of the pocket. Pin in position on the garment, lining side up, with the raw edge of the flap at the bottom, 1.5 cm (⅝ in.) above the top of the patch pocket. Tack in place along the raw edge, turning under the seam allowance as you go, and then stitch. Turn the flap down and press lightly, placing a cloth between the flap and the iron.

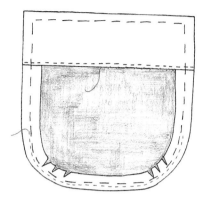

An unlined patch pocket is hemmed along the top edge and has the other edges turned under and basted in place. It is then stitched in place around the side and bottom edges.

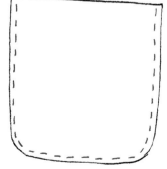

The flap is the same width as the finished pocket.

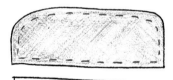

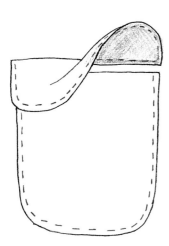

The flap is attached to the garment just above the pocket and then hangs down over it.

This unlined patch pocket has a ribbon trim for added interest – and no flap.

SLASHED POCKETS

Also sometimes called set-in pockets, these are fitted into an opening that has been made by cutting the fabric. The opening is then hidden or edged, and in doing so a feature is made of the pocket.

- A welt pocket has a fabric piece, like a stand, that extends above the pocket.
- A flap pocket has a flap that extends over the opening.
- A bound pocket has the edges in the opening finished neatly with bias binding.

The welt, flap, or binding will generally be made from the same fabric as the pocket. The inner pocket can be made from either the same fabric, or, as a lightweight alternative, lining fabric.

Welt pockets

For a welt pocket, mark the intended opening of the pocket, and baste or tack along it.

Make two identical pocket pieces (though one can be in lining fabric if you wish). Their top edges should be the same width as the intended opening.

Make the welt by folding a strip of fabric in half and trimming to slightly more than the width of the pocket opening. With right sides together, stitch across the ends. Trim the seam allowance and turn right side out. Press, placing a cloth between the fabric piece and the iron. Top stitch if you want to, on the enclosed sides.

Pin the welt piece to the right side of the fabric, beneath the intended opening, with the raw edge at the top of the piece and close to the basting stitches that mark the intended opening. Baste along the seam line.

Pin one pocket piece to the garment, with right sides together. The welt will be sandwiched between them. Match up the markings for the opening accurately. The top edge of the pocket will match the bottom edge (the raw edge) of the welt piece.

Turn the garment over to the wrong side and stitch around the intended opening, along both sides and with reinforcing stitches at each end. Slash between the stitching lines, stopping 1 cm (⅜ in.) before each end. Clip into the corners, as for a bound buttonhole (see p.62).

Pull the pocket piece through the slash, and baste around the opening. Press the welt into an upward position so that it covers the opening.

On the inside of the pocket, stitch the second pocket piece to the first, working around the edge.

On the right side of the garment, secure the welt using tiny stitches in matching thread.

A welt pocket is like a flap that stands up. It hides the opening to a pocket that lies on the inside of the garment.

Two fabric pieces are sewn together to form a pocket on the inside of a garment. On the outside a welt or a flap may conceal the opening to the pocket.

Flap pockets

For a flap pocket, mark the position of the intended opening with a row of basting stitches.

Cut a flap section the width of the pocket opening. Cut a facing piece the same size. Sew the flap to the facing with right sides together, leaving the base edge unstitched. Trim the seam and turn the flap right side out. Baste a row of stitches close to the stitched edge, having rolled the seam slightly to the side of the facing.

Pin the flap to the right side of the garment, above the intended opening, with the raw edge at the bottom and close to the basting stitches that mark the opening. Baste along the seam line.

On one pocket piece, mark the length of the opening. Place the pocket piece over the intended opening with the marked line matching the basting stitches on the fabric. (The flap will be sandwiched between them.) Pin and baste in position.

Turn the garment over to the wrong side and stitch around the seam line, along both sides and with reinforcing stitches at each end. Slash between the stitching lines, stopping 1 cm (⅜ in.) from each end. Clip diagonally into the corners.

Draw the pocket piece through the slash to the wrong side. Fold up the lower section of the pocket, forming a welt at the bottom edge of the opening, wide enough to fill the space and the marking pleats on the inside. Stitch the welt in position close to the seam line at the lower edge of the opening. On the inside, stitch the ends of the welt, catching the small triangles made by the diagonal cuts.

On the right side, press the flap section down over the welt. Turn the garment over to the wrong side and stitch the second section of pocket to the first section around the edges.

Topstitch the flap and then pin and baste it to the garment so it is pointing upwards. (When completed, it will hang down.)

This flap reveals the opening to the pocket, which can be made of lining fabric or self-fabric.

Bound pockets

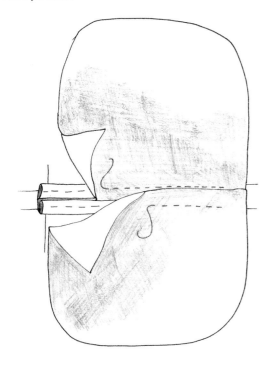

A bound pocket is 'bound' by two strips which edge the slashed opening. Pocket pieces cut from lining fabric are sewn with the right side of the garment facing up and the fabric binding in place, close to the raw edge of the binding and with pocket pieces placed as shown.

They are then pushed through to the wrong side of the garment and sewn together so that the bottom edges match and a pocket piece is formed. A rouleau loop adds decoration.

IN-SEAM POCKETS

An in-seam pocket is usually cut from lining fabric. For one pocket, cut two identical pocket pieces.

On the seam line of both garment pieces, where you will attach the pocket, mark the length of the opening. With right sides together, pin one pocket piece to the front seam allowance and stitch in place. Pin the other pocket piece to the back seam allowance and stitch in place. Press the pocket seams towards the pocket. Tack the two pocket pieces together along the opening and around the remaining raw edges.

Pin the garment pieces with right sides together along the seam above and below the pocket opening. Stitch these seams, reinforcing the stitching at the top and bottom pocket markings. Stitch the pocket pieces together around the curved edges.

Clip the back seam allowance at the top and bottom of the pocket to the stitching line and press the pocket section towards the front of the garment. Remove the tacking on the seam line to create the opening for the pocket.

The pocket that is set into the seam looks like this.

The opening for the pocket is unnoticeable in the seam.

TIP   THESE IMPORTANT POINTS ARE WORTH REMEMBERING WHEN
MAKING POCKETS:

▸ TAKE CARE MARKING WHERE THE POCKETS ARE TO GO, AND KEEP THEM
   SYMMETRICAL IF THERE ARE TWO (FOR EXAMPLE, ONE ON EACH SIDE OF A
   DRESS OR SKIRT).
▸ KEEP ALL CORNERS AS ACCURATE AS POSSIBLE.
▸ MAKE SURE THAT WELTS AND FLAPS ARE EVEN.
▸ ANCHOR THE EDGES OF FLAPS AND WELTS INVISIBLY TO THE GARMENT.

COLLARS

There are many styles of collar to choose from, and in this section instructions are given for making and applying the two main types: flat collars and collars with a stand.

The easiest collars to make, flat collars can have rounded or pointed corners. A so-called Peter Pan collar is a flat collar with a rounded edge.

Tailored shirts and blouses will usually have a collar with a stand. The collar itself turns down at the top of the stand and can be a variety of shapes. Most collars are cut in one piece, and most need interfacing to give them body and make them less flimsy.

Collars have to be attached with care. As with all finishing touches, these features will make or break the overall look of the garment.

FLAT COLLARS

It helps if you use a pattern piece for a collar, but you can make a flat collar by carefully tracing the shape of your neckline and making a collar piece and an undercollar piece, both of which are exactly the same shape.

Making a round collar

To construct a round collar, you will need a collar piece, an undercollar (which is the same shape and often the same fabric as the collar) and an interfacing.

Baste the interfacing to the wrong side of the undercollar. With right sides together, stitch two sections of the collar together, pivoting at the corner, and leaving the neck edge open.

Trim the interfacing close to the stitching. Clip small notches into the seam allowance, up to but not through the seam line.

Using the tip of the iron, press open the seam. Turn the collar right side out.

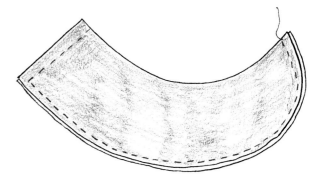

Stitch the collar and the undercollar with right sides together.

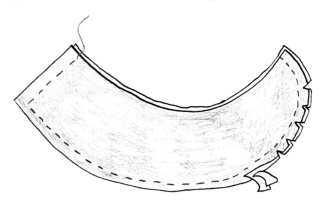

Clipping the curve will help the fabric lie flat.

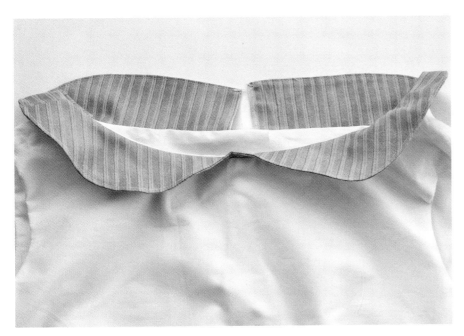

This is a Peter Pan collar.

TIP   WHEN CONSTRUCTING ANY COLLAR, USING A PRESSING CLOTH WHEN YOU PRESS IT IS IMPORTANT. ROLL THE OUTER SEAM JUST SLIGHTLY TO THE UNDERSIDE OF THE COLLAR, SO THAT THE SEAM WILL NOT SHOW AT THE EDGE OF THE COMPLETED COLLAR.

Understitch (see p.124) the seam allowance to the undercollar section, to prevent it from rolling to the outside. To understitch, open out the undercollar and stitch it to the seam allowance, close to the seam.

Press the collar flat and baste around the outer edge.

Making a pointed collar

To construct a pointed collar, you will need a collar piece, an undercollar (which is the same shape and often the same fabric as the collar) and an interfacing.

Baste the interfacing to the wrong side of the undercollar.

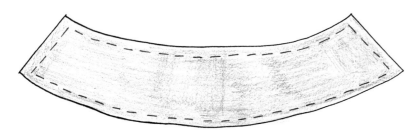

When you construct a flat collar, whether pointed or rounded, it will either be cut as one piece and then interfaced and folded, or cut as two pieces and then interfaced and basted together. This is how a pointed collar would look at the stage where it is all basted together.

With right sides together, stitch two sections of the collar together, leaving the neck edge open. To do this, start at the neck edge and stitch to the point. Take one diagonal stitch at the point and then continue stitching.

Trim the interfacing close to the stitching. It is essential to trim seams to reduce bulk, and clip curves to help seam allowances lie flat. Cut diagonally across the points within the seam allowance.

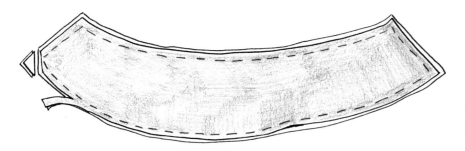

Grading seams (see p.124) and cutting off points reduces bulk.

Press the seam open. Turn the collar right side out and pull out the corners so that you have a fine point on each.

Understitch the seam allowance to the undercollar section. Press the collar flat and baste around the outer edge.

TIP   DO NOT USE THE POINT OF A PAIR OF SCISSORS TO POKE OUT THE CORNERS, AS IT IS ALL TOO EASY TO POKE A HOLE IN THE FABRIC. USE A BLUNT OBJECT SUCH AS A ROUNDED KNITTING NEEDLE INSTEAD.

Making an all-in-one collar and undercollar

An all-in-one collar and undercollar are cut out as one piece, which will be folded down the middle. Baste interfacing to the wrong side of the undercollar with one edge of the interfacing on the fold line. Fold the collar in half and, with right sides together, stitch the side seams. Trim the interfacing and trim diagonally across the points at the folded edge. Turn right side out, pull out the corners and press. Baste around the outer edges.

This is how an all-in-one collar would look as a cut-out fabric piece.

Applying a flat collar with self-facings

Stay stitch (see p.28) the neck edge of the garment. Pin the collar to the neck edge with right sides together. Tack in place.

Finish the garment front opening edges, which will form self-facings. Turn each self-facing to the outside along the fold line, and baste at the neck edge. The facing will overlap the ends of the collar.

Cut a bias strip 2.5 cm (1 in.) wide and baste to the edge over the collar, lapping the bias strip over the self-facings by about 2.5 cm (1 in..). Clip the curve at intervals. Turn the facings to the inside. Press the seam allowances towards the bodice. Turn in the free edge of the bias strip, and slip stitch to the bodice.

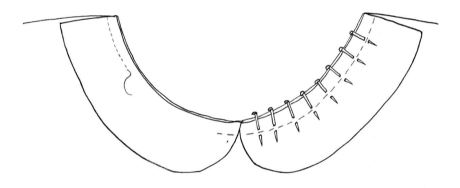

This is the first stage of applying a flat collar – you will need to pin first before tacking and then stitching.

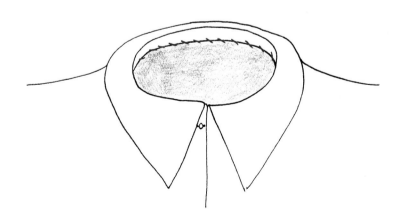

A pointed collar without a stand would look like this.

Applying a flat collar with a separate facing

Stay stitch the neck edge of the garment and of the facings. Pin and tack the collar to the neck edge of the bodice with right sides up.

With right sides together, pin and stitch the back facing to the front facings at the shoulder seams. Press the seams open. Finish the outer edge of the facing.

With right sides together, pin the facing to the bodice at the neck edge, matching the centres and sandwiching the collar in between. Tack and then stitch the entire neck edge. Clip the curve at intervals.

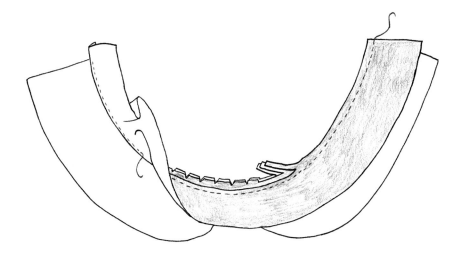

The collar is laid flat on the fabric, right side up, before the facing, right side down, is attached. Clipping, pressing and turning it to the inside of the garment gives the collar a neat edge

Press the seam allowance towards the facing. Understitch the facing (see p.124). Turn the facing to the inside, and press. Hand sew the facing to the shoulder seams of the bodice.

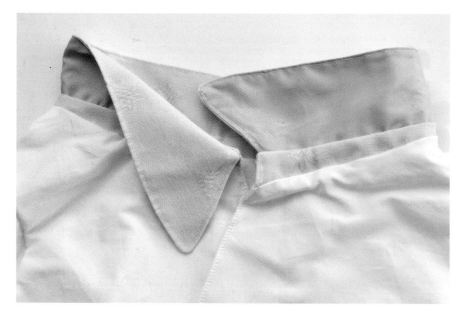

This collar is made with a separate stand.

MAKING AND APPLYING A COLLAR WITH A STAND

Prepare the collar as you would a flat collar (see p.73).

For the stand you need two identical pieces. Interface one of them. Turn in the seam allowance on the lower edge of the other stand piece; tack. Trim the seam allowance to about 5 mm (¼ in.).

Place the interfaced stand piece right side up on your work surface. Lay the collar on top of it, interfaced side down and raw edges even. Place the other stand piece, wrong side up, on top, again with the raw edges even. Pin and tack the collar in place. Machine stitch the tacked seam.

Press the stand away from the collar, using a pressing cloth for this to avoid making the fabric shine.

Stay stitch the neckline and clip into the seam allowance on the curve. Complete the front edges of the garment. Now pin, tack and stitch the interfaced side of the stand to the right side of the garment neckline. Trim the seam allowance and clip into the seam allowance on the curves. Press the seam towards the stand.

Pin the other side of the stand to the inside of the neck, just covering the seam. Slip stitch in place. Remove tacking. If you wish, topstitch around the stand close to the edges.

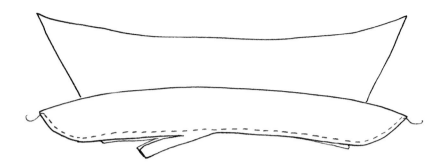

The edge of the collar is sandwiched between the front and back of the collar stand.

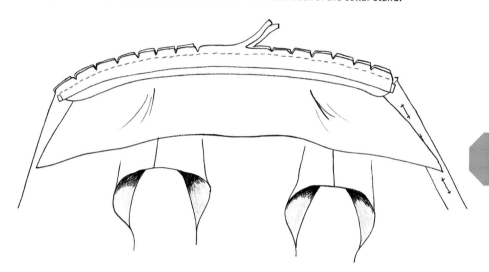

Grade and clip the seam (see p.124) that you have created by stitching the collar stand to the garment neck edge.

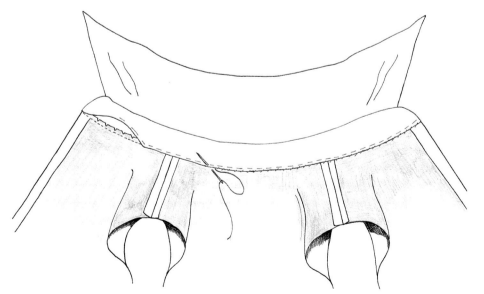

A slip stitch or other unnoticeable hand stitch is used to secure the collar stand to the inside of the shirt or blouse.

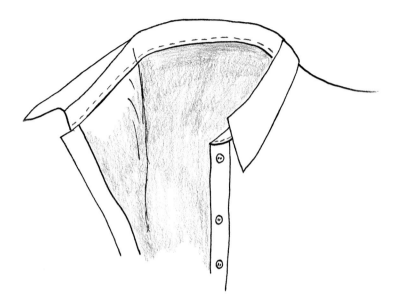

Most shirts feature a collar with a stand.

SHAWL COLLAR

This type of collar consists of a collar and lapels, cut from one pattern piece. The collar has a roll and can have a curved, scalloped or notched edge. You see shawl collars on coats, jackets and dresses.

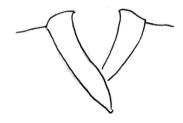

CUFFS AND SLEEVE CLOSINGS

Cuffs in all their styles and varieties add a design detail that never goes out of fashion. A cuff is either cut with the sleeve piece and turned back or added as a separate piece. The extended cuff, which is cut as a separate piece, adds length to the sleeve. The turned-back cuff rolls back to cover the base of the sleeve and is often a solely decorative feature.

Cuffs are given stiffness with an applied interfacing. They can have an opening or no opening. If the cuff has an opening, it may require a fastening.

If you are using a commercial pattern, a shaped cuff piece will be part of the pattern, but it is possible to add on a cuff without having a pattern piece.

TURNED-UP CUFF

This type of cuff can be any shape – but for the purpose of explaining how to apply a turned-back cuff, this one is straight and fits close to the sleeve.

If you are not using a pattern piece, cut a fabric piece twice the depth that you want the cuff to be, plus two seam allowances, and as long as the circumference of the sleeve plus two seam allowances. Pin and stitch the ends of the cuff and press it open.

Cut the interfacing to the same length and half the width of the fabric cuff piece. Pin and stitch the ends of the interfacing using a lapped seam.

A simple turned-back cuff looks good in contrasting fabric.

Pin the interfacing to the lower half of the cuff on the wrong side, with one edge along the fold line. Baste along both long edges. Turn right side out and press.

To apply the cuff to the sleeve, turn the sleeve wrong side out and place the cuff inside it with all raw edges even and right sides together. Stitch through all layers: sleeve (on top), top layer of cuff and interfacing. Press the seam open. Fold the cuff to the turned-up position.

Press, placing a cloth between the fabric and the iron. Unfold the cuff again so that it is no longer lying flat on the sleeve. Turn under the free edge of the cuff and slip stitch it over the seam. Turn up the completed cuff and press.

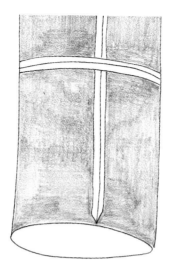

This shows the cuff section stitched into a ring, and applied to the lower edge of the sleeve, right sides together.

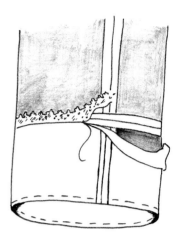

This is the newly applied cuff, turned back. Binding or lace can be added on the inside to cover the raw edge of the seam.

Here, the cuff is shown turned back, ready to wear, with the lace trim just showing on the inside of the sleeve.

This turned-back cuff is shaped, edged with bias binding and fastened with a button, in order to demonstrate the options you have for making a feature of a cuff, or putting a cuff on a sleeve that does not have one.

BAND CUFF WITH PLACKET

Shirt sleeves are finished with a placket and a band cuff that is fastened with press studs or buttons.

Before stitching the underarm seam of the sleeve, make the placket. Start by marking the opening in the sleeve, and then reinforce it by stay stitching a tall, narrow triangle with the marked opening down the middle. Slash along the mark.

To bind the placket, cut a strip of self-fabric 5 cm (2 in.) wide and twice the length of the placket. Open out the slash so that it is straight, and pin the fabric strip to the opening with right sides together. Stitch 3 mm (⅛ in.) from the edge, tapering to the end of the slash. Press the seam away from the sleeve. Turn under 3 mm (⅛ in.) along the free edge of the fabric strip and slip stitch it to the seam line.

Stitch the sleeve seam and press it open. Stitch two lines of gathering stitches along the lower edge of the sleeve.

Cut a piece of interfacing that is the same width as the cuff but half the depth. Baste it to the wrong side of the cuff, with one edge of the interfacing at the cuff fold line.

Fold the cuff along the fold line with right sides together; stitch the ends. Turn the cuff right side out and press.

Pull up the gathering stitches on the sleeve edge to fit the cuff, distributing the gathers evenly. Turn the sleeve wrong side out. Place the sleeve inside the cuff with right sides together, and stitch the lower edge through the sleeve (on top), the top layer of cuff and the interfacing. Press the seam towards the cuff.

Turn under the free edge of the cuff, and slip stitch it over the seam. Topstitch if desired.

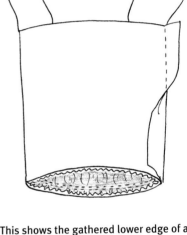

This shows the gathered lower edge of a sleeve ready to be stitched onto the band cuff. (It is illustrated with the sleeve turned right side out.)

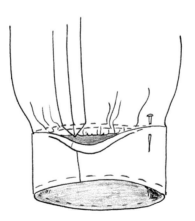

After the band is stitched to the sleeve edge, the remaining edge of the cuff is turned under and slip stitched to the inside of the sleeve.

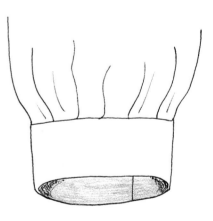

This is the completed band cuff attached to the gathered sleeve.

SLEEVE WITH CLOSING USING SEAM BINDING

As an alternative to a turned-up or band cuff, you can simply hem the edge of the sleeve, but if you need an opening to be inserted in the seam, do this before hemming the bottom edge of the sleeve.

Unpick the seam until the gap is 10 cm (4 in.) long. Press open the seam.

Cut two pieces of seam binding (or a matching or contrasting fabric) 2.5 cm (1 in.) longer than the opening. Turn under 12.5 mm (½ in.) at each end of one piece of seam binding. Pin this binding to the right side of one raw edge of the opening, overlapping the edge. Stitch 3 mm (⅛ in.) from the edge. Repeat with the other piece of binding on the other raw edge of the opening.

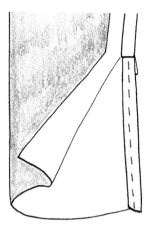

An opening made in a sleeve can be neatly finished with seam binding covering each of the two raw edges.

Clip into the back seam allowance just above the opening, and press the back seam allowance to the front above the clip. Turn the front edge of the opening to the inside along the seam line, and pin. Turn the back edge of the opening to the inside along the binding edge. Press and then slip stitch the edge of the seam binding to the sleeve at the front and the back.

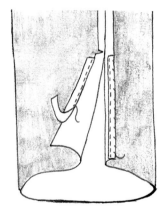

The second piece of binding will overlap the first – they will not meet edge to edge.

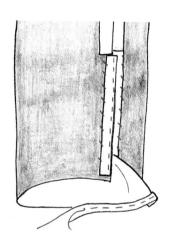

After the opening is bound, the sleeve lower edge can be hemmed using the same binding tape.

To finish the lower edge of the sleeve, cut a length of seam binding 2 cm (¾ in.) longer than the lower edge of the sleeve. Turn under slightly less than 1 cm (⅜ in.) at each end of the binding. Pin and stitch the binding to the right side of the sleeve edge, then turn it to the inside of the sleeve and press flat. Turn up the hem on the sleeve edge and slip stitch the binding to the sleeve on the wrong side.

Overlap the edges of the opening to the seam line. Sew press studs (see p.63) along the opening. Or, instead of press studs, thread loops can be sewn along the front edge of the opening on the right side, and small buttons on the back opening edge.

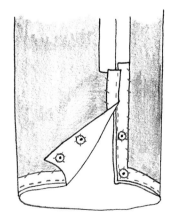

Press studs add a fastening to this opening.

SLEEVE WITH CLOSING USING ROULEAU LOOPS

This closing is similar to the closing using seam binding, but it uses fabric instead of seam binding, and so the long raw edges have to be dealt with. The loops are sewn on prior to the binding being attached.

Before hemming the bottom edge of the sleeve, unpick the seam until the gap is 10 cm (4 in.) long. Press open the seam.

Pin rouleau loops (see pp.64–5), pointing away from the edge, to the front edge of the opening on the right side of the fabric. Baste along the seam line.

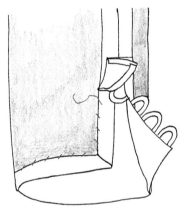

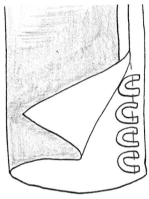

Tape with mitred corners has been used to neaten the inside of this sleeve with rouleau loops.

Make rouleau loops and sew these to the front edge of the opening, working with the sleeve turned wrong side out.

> TIP   WHEN MAKING CUFFS, THE MOST IMPORTANT CONSIDERATIONS ARE THE FIT OF THE CUFF ON THE BAND, AND THE FINISHING, INCLUDING CAREFUL PRESSING. ALL SEAMS SHOULD BE PRESSED TOWARDS THE CUFF.

Cut a strip of bias fabric 4.5 cm (1¾ in.) wide (or seam binding or tape if you prefer) and as long as the distance around the opening and around the lower edge of the sleeve, plus extra for turning under at the ends. Turn under both ends of the strip.

Starting at the top of the opening, pin and tack the strip, right sides together, over the loops on the right side of the front edge of the opening. Continue around the lower edge of the sleeve and finally along the back edge of the opening, creating a neat mitre (see p.90) at each corner. Now stitch all the way around, 3 mm (⅛ in.) from the edge.

Clip into the back seam allowance just above the opening, and press the back seam allowance to the front above the clip. Turn the front edge of the opening to the inside along the seam line, and pin. Turn the back edge of the opening to the inside along the binding edge. Turn under the raw edges of the binding, and slip stitch to the wrong side of the sleeve along both opening edges and the lower edge.

Overlap the opening, and mark the positions of the buttons through the centre of each loop. Sew on the buttons at the markings.

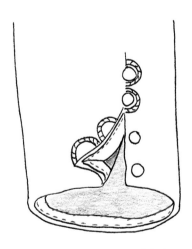

Be sure to check the position of the buttons as you sew them on, to make sure the loops will fit neatly over them.

SLEEVES

Sleeves need to feel comfortable and look good, showing no pull or strain on the garment. For a sleeve that meets these two vital specifications, work on the preliminary fitting. The comfort of the sleeve depends on a good fit at the shoulder and also having room for the elbow to bend. Make sure the sleeve is wide enough for your arm – it is worth making a toile (see p.106) just for this purpose. As with most construction techniques, pressing at each stage gives the end result a crisp, tailored look.

The sleeve that you will probably make most often is the set-in sleeve. Other kinds of sleeves include the kimono sleeve (cut as one with the garment piece) and the raglan sleeve (which joins the bodice in a diagonal seam extending to the neckline).

TIP   COMPLETE THE SLEEVE FINISH – HEM IT AND PRESS IT – BEFORE PERMANENTLY SETTING IN THE SLEEVE.

LEFT TO RIGHT **Set-in sleeve, raglan sleeve, kimono sleeve.**

Sleeves can be all different lengths. Cap sleeves are shorter than short sleeves, and either of these types is great for summer and also comfortable for garments worn under other clothing. Fashion sometimes dictates above-elbow length or three-quarter length, but wrist-length is always in style.

SET-IN SLEEVES

All set-in sleeves are cut with a sleeve cap that is fuller than the armhole section into which it is inserted. The fullness is necessary as it allows for movement of the arm, and therefore comfort to the wearer. In order for the sleeve to fit into the armhole, the extra fabric must be distributed evenly so that the fullness does not have the appearance of gathers. Do not rush to insert a sleeve until you are certain that it won't constrict your movement when you are wearing the garment. Try on the sleeve after you have basted it in position, and make adjustments as necessary before stitching.

Make the sleeve before inserting it but don't hem the lower edge until you have basted it in place and then tried it on.

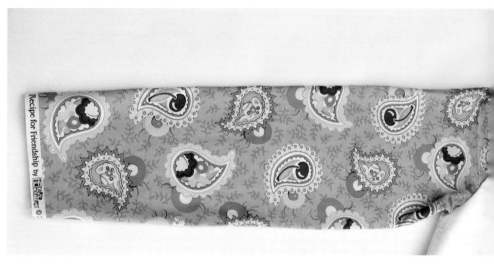

Basic set-in sleeves

Start by stay stitching around the sleeve cap first. Now stitch two rows of gathering stitches within the seam allowance between the markings on the sleeve cap, to be used as ease stitching.

Stitch the underarm sleeve seam.

With right sides together, pin the sleeve into the armhole, matching the underarm seams and matching the centre point of the sleeve to the shoulder seam. Also match any other marks – there are usually markings on sleeve pieces and bodice pieces that are to be matched, so always look for these when you pin the sleeve into the armhole.

Gently pull up the bobbin threads to reduce the length of the sleeve cap marginally. There should not be any pleats or gathers in the sleeve cap. Baste, and then try on the garment. Assuming it fits, you can now finish the lower edge of the sleeve (see pp.78–82).

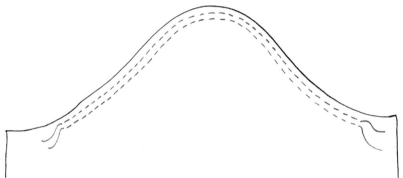

After the sleeve cap is stay stitched, two rows of gathering stitches are stitched between the markings.

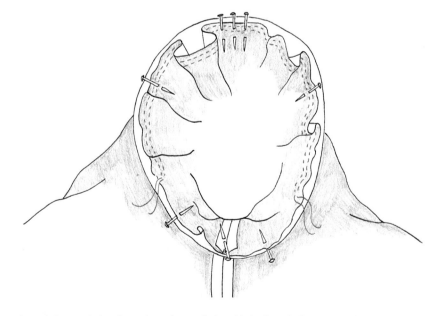

Pin and then tack the sleeve into the armhole. This is done before you pull up the gathering threads. This picture shows looking into the armhole with the sleeve pushed through.

Press on the wrong side of the fabric around the armhole to help it fit well. Working from the wrong side of the fabric, stitch the sleeve into the armhole with the sleeve uppermost on the machine.

Now stitch again, 5 mm (¼ in.) from the first stitching, within the seam allowance. Trim the seam allowance close to this stitching. Turn the seam allowance towards the sleeve, but do not press it.

Puffed sleeves

This is similar to a basic set-in sleeve but it has a gathered cap and so is easier to insert into the armhole.

Stitch the underarm sleeve seam. Sew two rows of gathering stitches within the seam allowance between the markings on the sleeve cap.

With right sides together, pin the sleeve into the armhole, matching the underarm seams and other markings. Draw up the bobbin threads evenly and distribute the fullness of the fabric to create gathers around the cap. Holding the sleeve towards you, baste the sleeve to the armhole, taking care to keep the gathers in place. Try on the garment. Assuming it fits, you can now finish the lower edge of the sleeve (see pp.78–82).

Working from the wrong side of the fabric, stitch the sleeve into the armhole with the sleeve uppermost on the machine. As you go, check that the gathers have remained even.

Now stitch again, 5 mm (¼ in.) from the first stitching, within the seam allowance. Trim the seam allowance close to this stitching. Turn the seam allowance towards the sleeve. Press with care to avoid flattening the gathers.

Shirt sleeves

This type of sleeve is constructed in a different way from other set-in sleeves. It is often used for men's shirts and is also useful on children's shirts.

Join the front of the garment to the back at the shoulder seams but do not stitch the side seams. With the garment laid out flat, pin the sleeve into the armhole, right sides together. It requires no ease stitching, as the sleeve cap is shallow. Baste and then stitch the armhole seam.

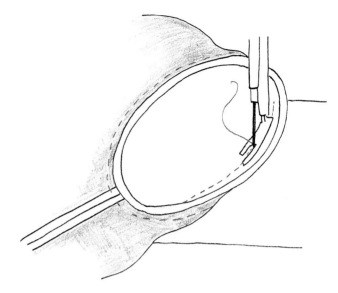

Work with the sleeve tucked inside the bodice of the garment as you machine stitch the armhole seam.

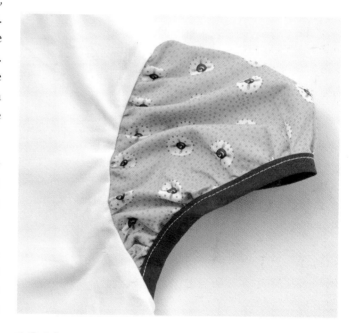

Puffed sleeves are often featured on children's clothes.

This seam can be treated as a flat fell seam (see p.35) or it can be stitched again, 5 mm (¼ in.) from the first stitching, within the seam allowance and then trimmed near the stitching.

With right sides together, pin the front to the back along the underarm seam and the side seam. Baste and then stitch as one continuous seam. Finish as for the armhole seam.

KIMONO SLEEVES

Part of a T-shaped garment, this is the simplest of all sleeves as it is cut as one with the bodice. It only works well, though, when the kimono sleeve opening is large, with a wide, draping sleeve. It is far less successful if the arm opening is smaller, as the fabric tucks and folds when the garment is worn. Reinforce the seams around the armhole by adding bias tape as this part of the garment takes the strain of the arm movement.

To stitch a kimono sleeve, pin the garment front to the back with right sides together, and stitch the underarm sleeve and side seam as one continuous seam. Clip into the seam allowance on the curve.

RAGLAN SLEEVES

This sleeve joins the garment in a seam that runs diagonally between the neckline and the underarm at front and back. Some shoulder shaping is necessary, and this is done with a dart or a shaped seam, which can be adjusted to suit your own arm and shoulder shape.

A raglan sleeve can be set into the armhole after the side seams of the garment have been stitched. Or, for a simple flat construction, you can stitch the raglan sleeve first, leaving the side seams of the garment open. If you choose the latter method, the raglan sleeve arm edges and the side seam of the garment can be stitched in one continuous seam, making sure the armhole seams match.

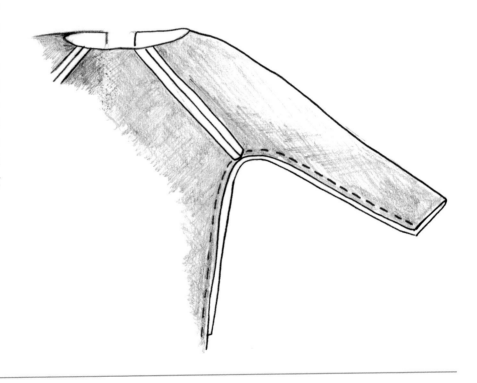

To make a raglan sleeve, sew the sleeve to the bodice before making this continuous seam, which joins the front and back of the top together at the side seams and goes on to become the underarm sleeve seam.

7 Finishing touches

IT IS OFTEN THE DETAIL OF A GARMENT OR ACCESSORY that people notice and admire. Take time to choose these finishing touches with care – and look for vintage lace, buttons and braid for something that will really make your creation different.

BIAS BINDING

Binding finishes and strengthens edges and is also a decorative trim. It can replace facings, but usually it finishes a hem, and it is also used for piping (see pp.91–2). Bias binding is cut on the bias of the fabric (unlike seam binding, which is cut on the straight grain). You can buy commercial bias binding, but the advantage of making your own is that you can use fabric that matches with your main piece.

MAKING BIAS BINDING

Fold the fabric diagonally so the lengthwise grain is parallel to the crosswise grain. Cut along the diagonal fold, which is the true bias of the fabric.

This shows the shape of the fabric when it has been cut along a diagonal fold.

Join strips by placing them at right angles to each other.

Decide on the width you'll need, which will be roughly twice the finished width plus two seam allowances. Measure and mark out lines parallel to the diagonal cut, the desired distance apart, so they are all exactly the same width. Cut out the strips, which will all have slanted ends.

To join strips, pin two strips with right sides together and at right angles to each other. Their slanted ends should be even but the more pointed corner of each needs to stick out beyond the other strip a little, so that the edges are exactly even at the seam lines.

Stitch the seam parallel to the slanted ends, on the straight of the grain of the fabric. Press open the seam and cut off the points that extend beyond the edges of the strip.

BINDING AN EDGE

You can bind an edge in either one stage or two. Whichever method you use, turn under the ends of the binding if you are starting and stopping at finished edges. Also, trim the seam allowance of the fabric so that it is slightly less than the finished width of the binding.

One-stage method

Prepare home-made binding by turning under both long edges along the seam lines, and then folding the binding lengthwise, with wrong sides together, so that the fold is slightly off-centre; press. (Commercial binding may already have some or all of these folds.)

Slot the edge into the folded binding with the wider side of the binding on the wrong side of the fabric. Pin, tack and then topstitch.

At **outer corners**, stop stitching at the edge. Take the binding around the corner, forming mitres (diagonal folds) at the corner on both the right side and the wrong side. Resume stitching at the inner corner of the binding.

At **inner corners**, first stay stitch for about 2 cm (¾ in.) each side of the corner, then clip diagonally into the corner up to the stitching. Pin just the narrower part of the binding in place. At the corner, fold the binding back on itself so the fold is even with the stitching line of the adjacent corner and the binding is tucked behind the adjacent side. Fold the binding diagonally to create a mitre, pin it, and then pin the narrow part to the new side. Turn the binding over to the wrong side and pin in place, folding it into a mitre at the corner on that side too. Tack and stitch through all layers.

Two-stage method

Pin one edge of the bias binding to the edge of the fabric, with right sides together and the seam lines aligned. (If you are using pre-folded commercial bias binding, open out the folded edge on the narrow side and align the fold with the seam line of the fabric.) Stitch the binding along the seam line.

Take the binding over to the wrong side of the fabric and pin, turning under the raw edge of the binding. If you don't want the stitching to show on the right side, slip stitch to the seam line. Otherwise, tack in place and then, working from the right side, machine stitch very close to the edge of the binding through all layers. Remove the tacking.

On an **outward corner**, stop the first stitching when you get to the seam line of the adjacent side. First fold the binding back to create a diagonal fold, then fold it again so the new fold is parallel to the first edge and the binding is now parallel to the adjacent edge. Pin and stitch. When you take the binding over to the wrong side, again fold it into a mitre at the corner.

On an **inward corner**, first stay stitch for about 2 cm (¾ in.) each side of the corner, then clip diagonally into the corner up to the stitching. Spread out the corner so that the two edges are no longer at right angles but are now in a straight line. With the fabric (rather than the binding) uppermost, pin and stitch along the seam line. On the right side, fold the binding into a mitre at the corner. Take the binding over to the wrong side, and fold it into another mitre on the wrong side; pin and stitch.

TIP   IF YOU ARE USING WIDE BINDING, IT'S A GOOD IDEA TO SLIP STITCH THE FOLD OF A MITRE TO KEEP IT IN PLACE.

FAR LEFT **If you make binding yourself, you can choose to use self-fabric or a patterned binding on a plain fabric or a plain binding on a patterned fabric.**

LEFT **Shop-bought bias binding like this satin one makes a neat finish to armholes, necklines and hems.**

PIPING

Piping is a folded strip of bias fabric that is inserted into a seam to make a decorative finish. Often it has cord inside it and is then technically called corded piping, but is often referred to simply as piping. Very thick corded piping is sometimes known as cording. Whichever name is used, it looks fantastic on cushions, pillows and bags of all sizes, as well as on necklines and waistlines.

The bias strips used for piping are generally cut from fabric, but you could use ribbon or even braid folded in half lengthwise. You can also buy ready-made piping. The cord that can be used for corded piping comes in various thicknesses.

MAKING CORDED PIPING

To make your own corded piping, cut and join together bias binding to make one long strip. Right side out, wrap this around the cord; pin in place with the raw edges even. Fit the zipper foot or piping foot on the machine, and baste close to the cord.

APPLYING PIPING OR CORDED PIPING

Pin the piping, facing inwards, to the right side of one fabric piece, placing the stitching on the piping just barely inside the seam line of the fabric piece. Clip into the seam allowance of the piping on curves and at corners.

TIP **To work out the width of the bias binding to use for corded piping, wrap a strip of fabric around the cord. You'll need this width plus two seam allowances.**

With the zipper foot or piping foot on the machine, baste along the seam line.

Where two ends of corded piping meet, unpick some of the tacking, pull back the fabric and trim the cord so that the ends butt up. Push the fabric back in place over the cord, turning under the end that is on top. Tack in place.

Place the other fabric piece on top of the first piece, right sides together, sandwiching the piping between them. Pin and tack. With the zipper foot or piping foot still on the machine, stitch along the seam line. Keep the stitching straight and the seam allowance exact so that the piping is the same width all along its length. Grade the seam allowances (see p.124). Press the seam allowances to one side.

Piping gives a professional look.

Piping can be made using either the same fabric or a contrasting one.

TIP   IF YOU HAVE TO JOIN TWO ENDS OF PIPING, TRY TO DO SO IN AN INCONSPICUOUS PLACE, AND NOT ON A CURVE OR CORNER.

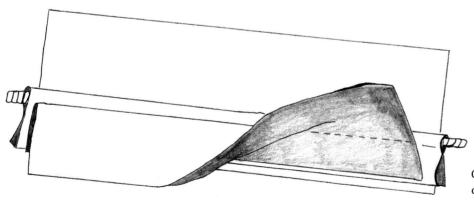

Corded piping is stitched between two edges of a seam so that it extends beyond the seam, creating a smart finish.

BRAID AND OTHER TRIMS

These add a lot of interest to either a garment or a household item. Choose trimmings that aren't too heavy for the fabric. Try to apply them before stitching seams. The fabric can then be laid flat, which makes it easier to work on, and it also allows you to hide the ends in the seams. If you cannot do this, turn under the ends as you attach them.

BRAID

This is used to outline a feature and as a border at a hem. You can buy braids in a variety of designs, textures, fabrics and widths. It has two decorative edges, and so is not inserted into a seam. Flat braid can be applied by hand with tiny invisible stitches in matching thread, or by machine. Sew careful topstitches near both edges of the braid if it is wide, or down the centre if it is narrow.

To mitre a corner, fold the braid back on itself. Pin and then stitch diagonally through all layers, from the outer corner up to what will become the inner corner. Trim the seam allowance of the mitre. Position the braid along the new edge, pin and continue stitching.

Fold-over braid can be used to finish raw edges. It is applied like the one-stage method of binding (see p.90).

RIBBON

Velvet, satin and grosgrain ribbons are suitable for trimming garments and household items like cushions, and ribbon makes a lovely appliqué. It is sewn on in the same way as braid.

Trims such as pompoms transform a plain piece and work particularly well on cushions.

DECORATIVE CORD

This is sewn onto the right side using tiny hand stitches, unless it is insertion cord, which has an attached seam allowance and is inserted into the seam in the same way as piping (see pp.91–2).

FRINGING AND OTHER EDGINGS

Edgings such as fringing have one decorative edge and one plain edge. They can be either applied as an edging to a hem or inserted into a seam using the same method as piping.

FEATHER TRIM

Also known as marabou, feather trim must be hand stitched in place around the central cord to which the feather is glued. Keep the stitches loose and fairly far apart when you attach it to an edge.

LACE EDGING

This comes in varieties such as **broderie anglais**, which is cotton lace and is often used on children's garments, **netted lace** which is used on lingerie and bridal wear, and **lace crochet**. All of these are best applied with hand stitches as they are delicate.

SEQUINS AND BEADING

Beading and sequins add a glamorous touch. Attach them singly or in a long strand. They are fiddly to sew on. Keep your thread shorter than the length of your arm to avoid a tangle, and do not pull stitches too tight. You may need a beading needle if the centre of the bead is tiny. It is best always to come from the back (underside) of the fabric, pushing the needle 1 cm (⅜ in.) through the fabric and slipping the sequin or bead onto the protruding needle tip. Secure the sequin in place by taking the needle through to the underside of the fabric once more, as close to the edge of the sequin as possible.

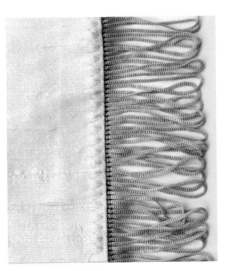

Fringing

Lace

Pompom

Feather trim

The hand beading on this dress by Juliette Barnes makes it unique.

Stitch on these embellishments before construction, and do not put them close to where a seam will be, because if beads get caught in the machine they can break the needle. When ironing, take care not to place the iron directly on beads and sequins, or they could melt.

TIP   BRAIDS AND OTHER TRIMS ARE MEANT TO ADD SOMETHING SPECIAL, BUT THEY CAN SPOIL THE LOOK OF WHAT YOU HAVE MADE. WHATEVER TYPE OF TRIMMING YOU ARE USING, THE MOST IMPORTANT THINGS TO REMEMBER ARE THESE:

- ▸ MARK ACCURATELY WHERE THE TRIM IS TO BE PLACED AND FREQUENTLY MEASURE TO CHECK THAT ITS IS PERFECTLY IN PLACE WHILE YOU APPLY IT.
- ▸ SELECT AN INCONSPICUOUS PLACE TO BEGIN AND END THE APPLICATION OF THE BRAID OR TRIM.
- ▸ APPLY IT WITH TINY INVISIBLE STITCHES AND BE SURE THAT THERE ARE ENOUGH TO MAKE THEM DURABLE.

RICKRACK

Cheerful and colourful, rickrack makes a traditional decorative border and looks effective in rows of two or more. It comes in different sizes and can be applied in three different ways.

Topstitching rickrack

Pin the rickrack to the right side of the fabric; tack. Stitch through the centre of the rickrack by machine, and remove tacking.

Attaching rickrack behind a hem

When rickrack is attached behind a hemmed edge, it forms a sawtooth edging. Fold the fabric to the back and press the edge. Now pin and stitch the rickrack behind the fabric so that half of it is visible from the front.

Rickrack is a popular decorative trim on children's clothes.

Rickrack comes in different sizes for different jobs. This is attached behind the hem.

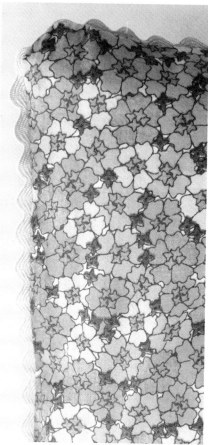

The rickrack inserted into the seams makes a decorative edge to this cushion.

Attaching rickrack in front of a hem

With this method, the half of the rickrack that extends beyond the edge creates a sawtooth edging, while all of the rickrack is visible. Fold back and press the hem. Pin the rickrack along the very edge of the hem on the right side; stitch in place.

Inserting rickrack in a seam

When inserting rickrack into a seam, place the rickrack on the right side of one fabric piece, centring it on the seam line. Place the second section of fabric on top of the first so that the right sides are together and the rickrack is sandwiched in between the two layers. Make the seam to join the two pieces. Open out the two sections to reveal the 'point design' piping.

ROSETTES

These decorative fabric rosettes can be used singly or in clusters of rosettes in different sizes and materials. They look stunning on fashion items, accessories and interiors alike.

For each rosette you will need a 75 x 14 cm (30 x 5½ in.) bias strip of fabric and an 8 cm (3 in.) circle, cut from the same fabric. On the circle, turn under a narrow hem (unless you are using felt), hand stitching it on the wrong side.

MAKE THE STRIP

Cut your strip of fabric on the bias. Trim both ends to make a pleasing curved shape. Your strip will look like a long ice lolly stick.

Now fold the strip in half lengthwise, with right sides together. Pin and stitch a 1 cm (⅜ in.) seam along the length of the strip leaving a 2 cm (¾ in.) gap at one end. Trim the seam allowance. Turn right side out through the unstitched gap using a blunt-ended knitting needle, so that you have a strip which resembles a fabric belt.

Machine stitch or hand sew a row of gathering stitches along the long edge of the strip on the same side as the seam. Pull the bobbin thread to gather the strip, with the gathers concentrated at one end, which will form the centre of a flower with tightly packed 'petals'.

Begin the rosette by sewing a folded strip of fabric with right sides together.

ROLL THE STRIP AND STITCH IT TO THE BASE

Begin rolling up the strip, starting at the tightly gathered end, and secure with hand stitches to the circular base as you go. Continue rolling and stitching to the end of the strip. As the rosette forms, you will see how you can determine the shape by gathering the fabric closer together so that the 'petals' effectively spread out. Keep stitching the gathered strip to the base as it takes shape.

For once you don't want even gathers along the whole length – keep the gathers tight at one end.

Sew the rolled-up strip to the circular base.

FINISH THE ROSETTE

With the strip secured on to the circular base, attach the outer edge with tiny stitches. Now sew the rosette to your chosen fabric with tiny hand stitches through the middle of the flower and the circular base.

These rosettes are decorative on a jacket, dress or bag.

BOWS

What looks like one long piece of fabric tied into a big, floppy bow is actually made up of one main piece that forms the two loops, a second piece forming the 'knot' and two separate (optional) long ends.

First decide on the size of your bow. A large bow looks good on the back of a dress at the waist – small bows decorate the shoulder or neckline. For the main piece (which will form the two loops of the bow), cut a rectangle of fabric that is twice the width by twice the length of the desired finished bow. For the central knot, cut a strip of fabric that is also twice as long as it is wide, and that is as long as half the width of the main piece. If you want to include the two long ends, cut four identical shapes, each as wide as the depth of the finished bow (excluding the long ends).

A bow with long ends is perfect on a door handle on an antique wardrobe.

A large organza hand-tied bow makes this dress by Natalie Williams special.

Create the bow piece by folding the main piece in half lengthways with right sides together. Pin and stitch a seam to create a 'tube' of fabric. Turn this tube right side out through the opening.

For the knot piece, fold the small strip in half lengthwise and then make it up in the same way as the main piece, forming a smaller tube.

For each of the two long ends (if using), pin and stitch two of the end pieces, with right sides together, around the two long sides and the bottom. Snip off the seam allowances at the corners. Turn right side out. Turn in the raw edges at the top and slip stitch.

Press all the pieces and then gather the bow piece by hand sewing gathering stitches down the centre of the shape, from one long edge to the other. Pull up the thread to gather the piece into a bow shape.

Cover the gathering stitches in the centre with the knot piece, wrapping it around the centre of the bow. Hand sew the ends of the knot piece together at the back. Sew the long ends, if using, to the back.

This simple bow has been made with two tubes of fabric.

8 Using commercial patterns

THE MOST IMPORTANT THING WHEN WORKING FROM A PATTERN is to take time reading. Read the envelope for important information such as selecting the correct size. Read the instruction sheet for information on laying out the pattern, cutting out, and making up the garment. And read the pattern pieces for additional information presented in a type of code – known as pattern markings.

READING THE PATTERN ENVELOPE

The image on the front of the pattern envelope is your guide to how the finished garment will look. Often there will be illustrations or photographs of different views of the same garment, taken from different angles. Some patterns have a few different items in the same pattern – say, three styles of dress.

On the back of the envelope are working drawings of the garment or garments. These are simple diagrams, showing where seams, darts and fastenings go, as well as information such as a size guide, how much fabric to buy, which fabrics are suitable and the 'notions' required. Notions are items of haberdashery, such as zips, thread and buttons. Also on the back of the pattern are important boxes of information, mainly about sizes and fabric quantities.

The box giving body measurements will indicate the exact measurements for bust, waist and hip for each size. The pattern manufacturers need to be specific here, as shop-bought clothes vary a great deal. One shop's size 10 may be the same actual size as another shop's 12. The garment measurement box will give the actual size of the finished garment, as well as the width of the skirt at the lower edge or the width of the trouser leg.

If you are buying fabric online, you will need to have read with care the recommendations on the pattern about how much fabric, and which type, is needed. If you like to see what you buy before you buy it, then a fabric shop or department in a big store will have experts to help you decipher the information on the back of the pattern, and will lead you to the choices of fabric available.

LEARNING THE JARGON AND DECODING SYMBOLS

On each of the pattern pieces there are markings such as lines, dots and arrows. Two of the most commonly seen are **grain line arrows** and '**place to fold line' arrows**. Arrows that indicate the grain line must match up to the grain in the fabric. A straight arrow must be placed on a straight grain. Bent arrows, which mean that the pattern piece must be placed on the fold of the fabric, will also have the instruction 'place to fold'.

The dark-ink line is the **cutting line**. For a single-size pattern the cutting line is appropriate to the size purchased. On a pattern that has cutting lines for a variety of sizes – a 'multi-size' pattern – the lines for each size are labelled, so be sure to follow the right line.

Large and small dots are printed on the pattern paper for accurate joining of garment sections. They are particularly helpful when you are matching stripes or where even distribution of gathers is required.

Notches are used for accurate joining of seams. Cut around the outside of them, and if it is a double notch cut around both as one wide notch.

Dart symbols need to be carefully matched. The broken lines that meet at a point show the size and shape of the dart and the line on which to stitch.

Fastening markings show the length of the opening that should be left in the seam in order to accommodate the zip.

The following markings are often seen.

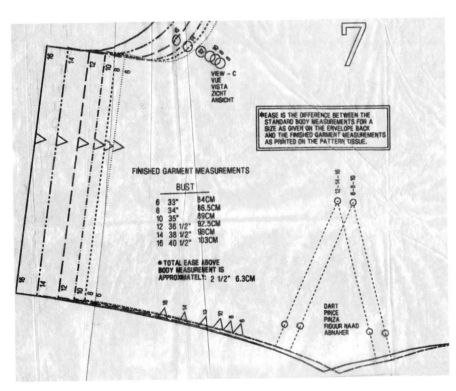

Here is a typical pattern piece on which you can see a selection of markings.

SORTING OUT THE PATTERN

Often the pattern you choose will have patterns for garments that you are not making, as well as the one you have selected. The style of your choice will be labelled – usually A, B or C. Take only the pieces marked C if the dress you are making is style C on the front of the pattern envelope. All pattern pieces for the style of your choice are listed by number, so for style C, say, you will have pieces that are each marked with a C and a number.

To identify the pieces, there will be a list of each pattern piece, the number the piece has been given, and a description of it – for example, centre front. This list will be found on the instruction sheet.

When you use the pattern for the first time, sort out the pieces you will need and put the rest neatly folded in the envelope.

Make sure you have all the fabric you need. You will find that some pattern pieces instruct you to cut the piece from lining as well as from the fashion fabric. Prepare yourself by having to hand all that you need.

Look at the instruction sheet and get familiar with where on the sheet you'll find the instructions relevant to you. It's helpful to mark the bits you will need to read when following the guide to cutting out and making up the garment, before doing either task.

Group together the pieces for the lining, for the interfacing and for the main fabric.

Check your measurements against those of the pattern pieces. If an adjustment is to be made to the paper pattern, now is the time (see p.106).

LAYING OUT THE PATTERN AND CUTTING OUT THE FABRIC

You will need a large, flat surface on which to lay out the pattern, cut out the fabric and mark the fabric and lining. A clean floor will be fine for laying out, while a table is better for cutting and marking.

Work out which is the right side and which is the wrong side of the fabric. This may seem obvious, but sometimes it is surprisingly difficult.

You will also need to see if the fabric looks different from one direction – with a pile or surface that can be smoothed in one direction only. If this is the case, the fabric is described as '**with nap**'. Because the fabric must be cut out so that the texture all lies the same way, you must use the 'with nap' layout instructions. Fabrics with a print that is a one-way design must also be cut with all the pattern pieces placed in the same direction. Treat these, as well as textured fabrics such as satin and brocade, as 'with nap' when laying out the pattern and cutting out the fabric.

TIP LAY THE PATTERN ON FABRIC WHICH YOU HAVE ALREADY WASHED AND PRESSED.

Take time to lay out your pattern with care.

Read the tips for economic layout of the pattern you have chosen to make. There will be a suggested plan of how to lay the pattern on the fabric in a way that doesn't waste fabric. Special consideration is needed when laying out a pattern on checked, striped or floral fabric – the patterns in checks and stripes need to match, and prints need to all go the 'same way'. Large prints may also need to match.

Place the pattern pieces on the right side of the fabric, with the printed side up unless the instructions on the layout guide tell you differently. Lay all the pattern pieces on the grain line as indicated. Your fabric is on the grain when crosswise and lengthwise threads are at perfect right angles to each other. Never skimp on fabric by putting pieces off the grain – the resulting garment will not hang as it should.

Some patterns will require you to cut out the fabric on the bias. To establish the bias line on the fabric, draw a lie at a 45 degree angle to the lengthwise grain. This line in the fabric will have the most stretch.

Where you see the bent arrow marking **'place to fold'**, place the line of the pattern piece on the fold, with no gap, and with the line parallel to the selvedge (one of the two finished edges of a woven fabric, on the lengthwise grain).

There will be an instruction for how many pieces to cut. If it says 'cut two', you will need to place the pattern piece on a double layer of fabric *with wrong sides of the fabric together.* If the pattern piece is to be placed on the fold of the fabric, you will cut out one piece, which, when unfolded, will be twice the size of the pattern piece.

- Lay out all the pattern pieces before cutting the first one out.

- When double layers are shown on the layout, fold the fabric with right sides together.

- Cut with straight scissors, not pinking shears, making sure the fabric is flat on the table.

- Don't forget to cut around notches and cut groups of notches as one for easy matching.

- Check the number of each piece you need to cut. Cut on the cutting line.

- Fold the cut pieces and keep them together, where possible leaving the pattern piece on the fabric.

- Use tailor's tacks (see p.13), chalk, dressmaker's carbon with a tracing wheel (if suitable for the fabric), or a running stitch – sometimes called thread tracing – to transfer markings to the wrong side of the fabric, while the pattern pieces are still attached.

- Scraps can be used for sections not cut from the pattern and for testing stitches – so do not throw them away.

Place the piece on the very edge of the fold.

Pin the patterns to the fabric every 5 cm (2 in.) or so, but to start with put in a few pins to hold the pattern in place.

Cut on a flat surface.

TIP   KEEP ONE HAND FLAT ON THE PATTERN PIECE AS YOU CUT.

COMMON ADJUSTMENTS TO THE PATTERN

If you are between two sizes, cut out the fabric between the two size lines. To make a minor change as you cut, such as making the waist smaller, cut to the larger size, and taper to the next size down at the waist. If you are at all unsure, cut the pattern 1 cm (⅜ in.) outside the cutting line. It is easy to make wider seam allowances to take in a garment slightly but impossible to make the pieces bigger once they are cut.

Sometimes you will find that your measurements and those on the paper pattern do not match, and alterations must be made on the pattern. A pattern will have a line to mark at which point you need to lengthen or shorten the pattern while still retaining the original shaping of the piece. Take advantage of these adjustment lines. Darts can also be repositioned and crotch length increased or decreased.

If you do these changes, don't forget to alter corresponding pieces such as the centre front lining piece and the facing for the piece. Also, all changes must leave the resulting pattern symmetrical – so a change to one side means the same change to the other.

The best way of achieving a perfect fit, is to make a **toile**. This is a mock-up of your garment, made in cheap fabric before you cut out your main fabric. By making a toile, you will be able to spot any fit problems and adjust the fit of the pattern before it is too late.

When trying on the toile, check that the lengths of sleeves and hems are right, the bust and waist darts are accurate, the shoulder of the blouse or top is sitting on your shoulder, and the skirt skims your hips without fitting too tightly or adding bulk if too large.

KEEPING PATTERNS IN ORDER

Be sure to be organised with your pattern pieces. Fold them away after use (trying to refold along the original creases makes it easier to get them back into the original envelope), and if returning them to the envelope is too tight a squeeze, use clear plastic folders and label them.

Search charity shops or the internet for vintage patterns, but read the sizes with care as they differ a lot.

9 Get sewing!

MAKE YOURSELF COMFORTABLE BEFORE YOU BEGIN! Wouldn't it be nice to have a sewing room? Imagine a spacious table with the sewing machine permanently set up, a pinboard for inspirational tear sheets from magazines, shopping lists and fabric swatches, a large flat cutting surface, storage for fabric and ongoing projects, a place for the ironing board, and even a mannequin.

Dream on! Not many of us can have all that is mentioned here, but it is important that you clear your dining table to cut out both patterns and fabrics and set your machine up where you have a little room to move, and good lighting.

Organise patterns, threads, haberdashery and fabrics on a shelf or in plastic boxes, and be prepared to have the iron set up, too, for each step of the construction. Have all the essentials to hand – scissors, tape measure, rulers and notions – and your prepared pattern pieces. Don't forget to wash your hands before you start handling your fabric.

Plan your sewing so that you can, if possible, complete one stage of construction each time you sew, and leave everything neatly stored, ready to go again. Organise the order of tasks you will undertake, using the pattern if you have one, or make a list for simple projects like cushion covers, tablecloths or even repair jobs. If you are making clothes without an instruction sheet, try using the 'Easy Steps to Making ...' (pp.109–23), which give the tried and tested order of events for simple garment construction.

EASY STEPS TO MAKING A LINED DRESS

For this you must make two complete dresses – one in your fabric and one
in lining fabric. Press each step as you go.

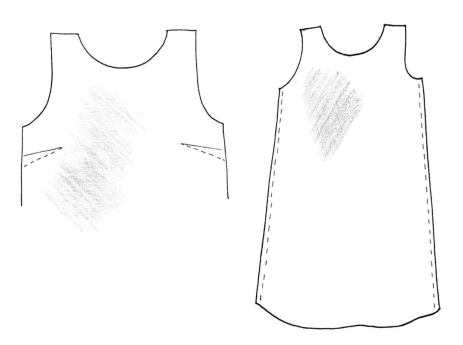

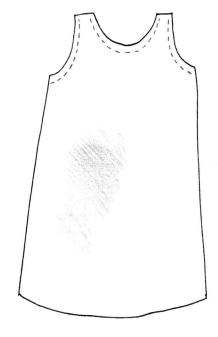

Sew the bust darts on both dress and lining.

Sew the side seams. Use a long stitch along
the side seam where you will insert the zip,
on both dress and lining.

Stitch the two dresses together, attaching
them around the neckline and armholes. The
right side of the dress fabric must be facing
the wrong side of the lining (if it has a right
and wrong side).

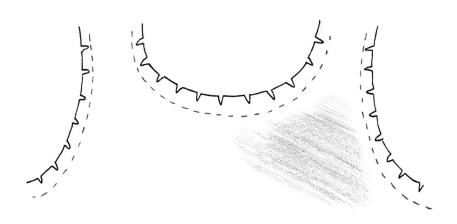

Clip into the seam allowance on the curve to
make it lie smoothly.

Hem both the dress and the lining
separately using a blind hemming or slip
stitch (shown) on the dress and a machine
stitch for speed on the lining.

Next pull the lining through the openings at the shoulders – and you will then have a lined dress.

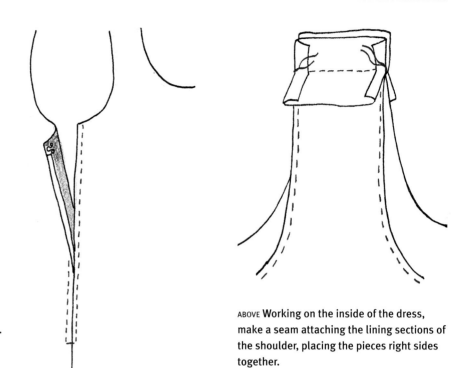

RIGHT Insert the zip behind the seam where you have sewn long stitches using a centred application (see pp.56–8) in the seam of the dress piece. Open the seam in the lining section to the same length, and finish the zip insertion by making a neat slip-stitched attachment of the lining fabric to the zip tapes. The zip sits in between the two layers: the dress and the lining.

ABOVE Working on the inside of the dress, make a seam attaching the lining sections of the shoulder, placing the pieces right sides together.

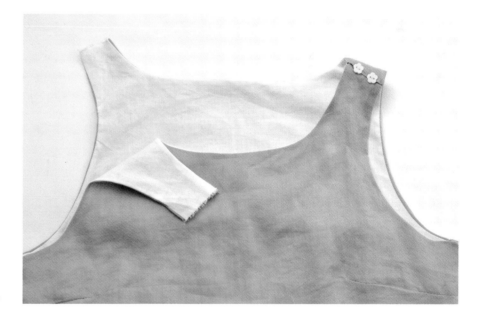

RIGHT The last step is to sew the shoulder seams together – you will need to hand sew here.

RIGHT Working on the outside of the dress, make a shoulder seam to attach the dress shoulder front to back by easing the two pieces together and slipping one inside the other with a slight overlap. Join by hand with a tiny slip stitch.

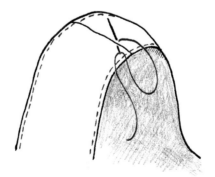

This simple dress is good on its own or over jeans.

EASY STEPS TO MAKING AN A-LINE SKIRT

This is an unlined skirt with a back zip.

Start with the darts at front and back.

This is the back of the skirt. Stitch the side seams, and stitch back seam using a long stitch where the zip will be inserted.

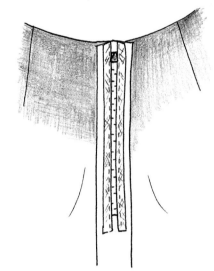

Insert the zip using centred application (see pp.56–8).

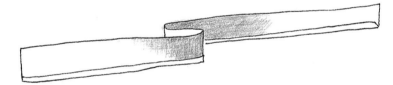

The waistband is made from a strip on which one edge is first turned under and then the strip will be folded in half lengthwise with right sides together.

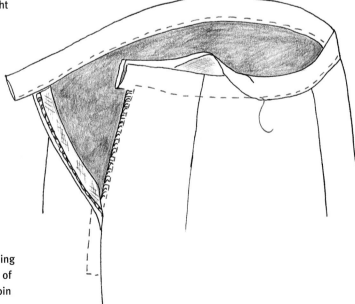

Working on the inside of the skirt, attach the waistband by stitching the right side of the waistband along one edge to the wrong side of the skirt waist edge. Bring the band to the front of the skirt and pin and tack into position before topstitching it.

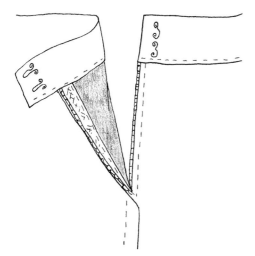

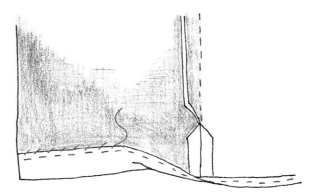

Finish the ends of the waistband by tucking the fabric into the inside and stitching with tiny invisible stitches. Next attach a hook and eye or press stud to close.

Hand hem to finish.

Back of skirt.

Make this skirt any length.

EASY STEPS TO MAKING A CHILD'S DRESS

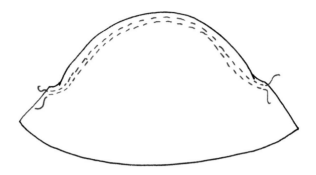

RIGHT **Prepare the sleeve by stitching gathering stitches to the upper edge.**

Sew seams at the shoulders.

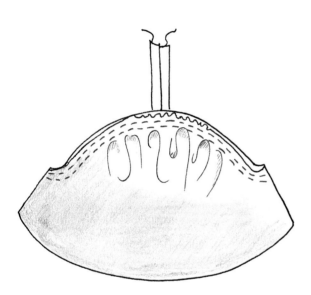

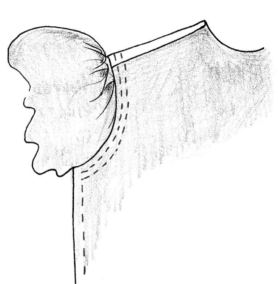

ABOVE **Ease the gathered sleeve to the armhole edge.**

ABOVE **Sew the underarm seams and bodice side seams, and sew the back seam of the bodice using long stitches along the seam where the zip will be inserted.**

RIGHT **Make a casing for elastic at the bottom edge of the sleeve. Insert narrow elastic and secure the ends of the elastic together using a machine stitch.**

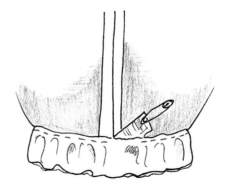

Gather the waist so that it fits the bodice and the gathers are even.

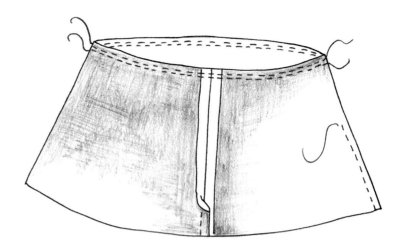

RIGHT Sew the side seams of the skirt, and sew the back seam using a long stitch along the part of the seam where the zip will be inserted. Prepare the top edge, which will be at the waist, with two rows of gathering stitches.

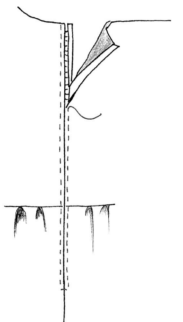

LEFT Having gathered the skirt to the appropriate size, attach the skirt to the bodice with right sides together. Insert the zip using centred application (see pp.56–8).

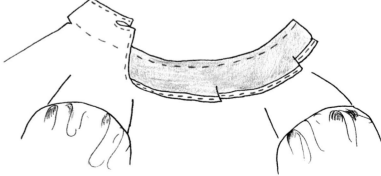

RIGHT Hem the bottom edge of the facings with a narrow machine-stitched hem. Finish the neckline by applying facings to both front and back. Do this by first sewing the front and back facings together and then applying them to the neckline with right sides together as you sew.

Add the frill (see p.42).

The frill is a traditional option for a child's dress.

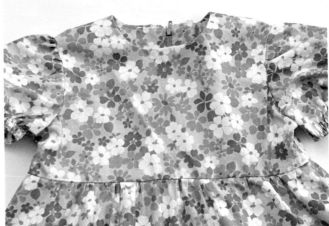

The facing gives the neckline a neat finish.

This dress can have a collar, a sash or any type of trim added if you want more going on.

EASY STEPS TO MAKING A NIGHTIE

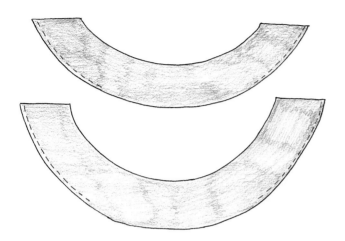

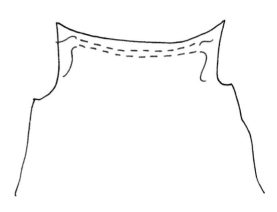

Prepare the front and back yokes by sewing them with right sides together between two markings – or if there are no markings, leave the curved bottom edge free as this attaches to the front piece. Clip the edges of seams and turn the yokes right side out. Gently press using a cloth between the fabric and iron.

Prepare to gather the front and back top edge of the nightie with two rows of gathering stitches.

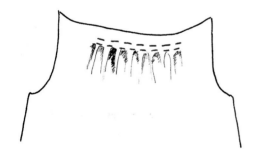

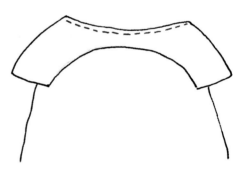

Gather up to the right length to fit the unstitched section of the yoke pieces.

With right sides together, attach the front yoke to the front of the nightie, and the back yoke to the back of the nightie. Do this by placing the yoke with the right side of the top fabric facing the right side of the nightie, with the edges even and the yoke hanging upside down. Stitch through two layers only – the nightie fabric and the layer of yoke that will form the right side of the fabric.

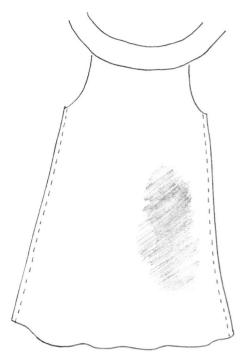

Stitch the side seams.

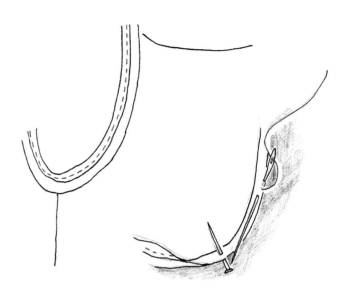

Finish the armholes with bias binding (see pp.88–90).

Working on the outside of the nightie, make a shoulder seam to attach the shoulder fronts to the shoulder backs by easing the two pieces together and slipping one inside the other with a slight overlap. Join by hand with a tiny slip stitch.

ABOVE Slip stitch is used frequently in garment construction.

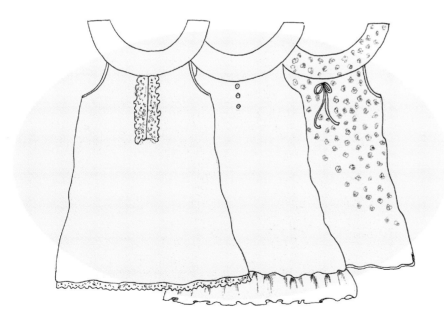

Binding can also be added to the hem, or lace or a frill to finish, as well as trims such as ribbon or buttons as a decorative feature.

This nightie has no fastenings – it just slips over the head.

Putting on that bit of ribbon is the most rewarding part!

TEN TIPS FOR PRESSING

1. Get the gear – a **sleeveboard** is for areas such as sleeves that are slim and hard to get to; a **tailor's ham** is for pressing round or curved shapes such as darts and sleeve caps; a **seam roll** is for long seams – it stops getting ridges on the right side of the fabric; a **pressing pad** is three or four layers of fabric such as towelling, used to provide thickness under where you are working, when pressing buttonholes, sequinned fabric and other raised surfaces.

2. Always use a pressing cloth.

3. Press on the wrong side of the fabric.

4. For a crisp edge hem, use a seam roll. For a soft edge hem, use just steam, or use the iron to pat the hem, never applying pressure.

5. Use the point of the iron when pressing gathers.

6. Use a tailor's ham when pressing darts.

7. To avoid ridges appearing on the right side of the fabric, put brown paper between the fabric layers when pressing the folds of darts, edges of pleats, welt or flap pockets and zip plackets.

8. Do not press over pins.

9. Never press sharp creases until you are sure they are where you want them. (Try on first to establish the right fit.)

10. Do not over-press!

EASY STEPS TO MAKING SIMPLE TROUSERS

Stitch the darts first.

Sew the front and back seams of the crotch with right sides together.

Stitch the front of the legs to the back of the legs with right sides together, using a long stitch along the seam where the zip will be inserted.

Next insert the zip using centred application (see pp.56–8).

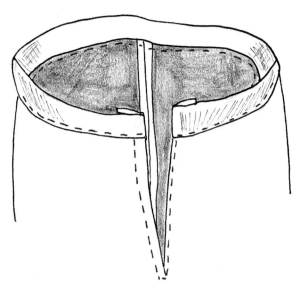

With the right side of the trouser waist lapped by the right side of the facing (or tape if desired), sew the facing to the waist and then fold it into the inside of the trousers so that a neat top edge is achieved.

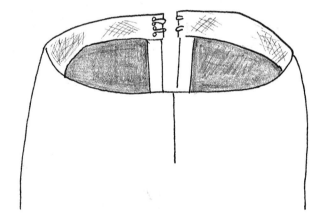

Add hooks and eyes or a metal hook to the facing and hem at the ankle to the desired length using a hand hemming stitch.

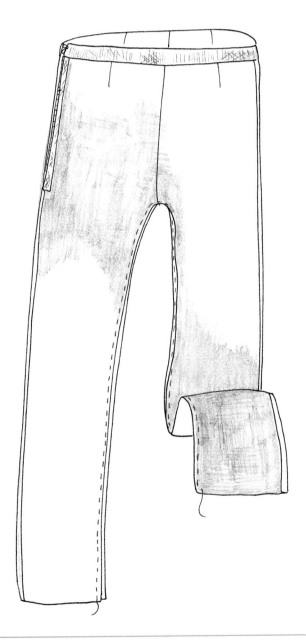

Stitch the inside seams of the trouser legs.

Trousers with a side zip and no waistband are easy to make.

MAKE YOUR SEWING LOOK MORE PROFESSIONAL

Of course practice really does help, but starting off aiming for accuracy in laying out pattern pieces and cutting and preparing fabric will make a big difference to the end result. In addition to taking your time to get it right, make sure you press every stage of the construction, and reduce bulk whenever you can. Lastly, you need to trim and clip away bulk for a neat finish – here's how.

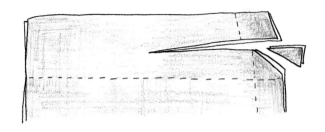

Snip off the seam allowance at corners.

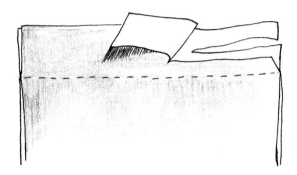

Grade seams by trimming each seam allowance by a slightly different amount, to lessen bulk.

Understitch facings on the inside – this means adding tiny stitching to secure the piece in place.

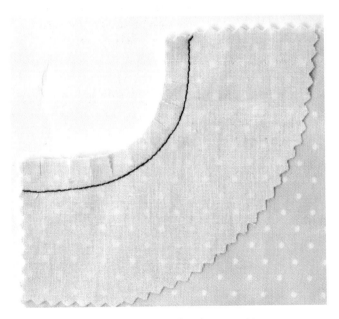

Clip as shown at curved edges to reduce lumps and bumps.

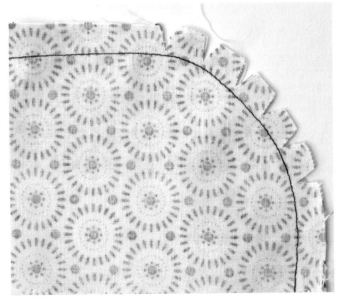

10 Giving old clothes a new look

REPAIRING, RECYCLING AND REMAKING CLOTHES is more than just making a fashion statement. Not many people would simply chuck out old clothes today. Most would take them to a charity shop or at least recycle the fabric, but it is possible, with imagination, to 'rework' the garment. It might be a simple repair to worn fabric, or you could replace a broken zip or maybe something that doesn't fit well can be remodelled so that it is just the right size. Changing a feature, such as removing a bow or adding a trim or buttons, can give an item a new lease of life. Or you could remake it totally, by combining two items to make one, as shown here. Happy reusing!

OLD CLOTHES – NEW TWIST

A SKIRT FROM JEANS

Cutting off the legs

Try on the jeans and make a mark with chalk about where you want the skirt length to be.

Take off the jeans and fold them with both legs together, matching the waist and legs perfectly.

Draw a line across where you have made the mark with chalk.

Cut off the legs of the jeans, making sure you cut the length to the mark and you cut dead straight.

Rip the seams

Using an unpicker if you have one, remove the seams from the remaining portion of the legs. Remove all threads.

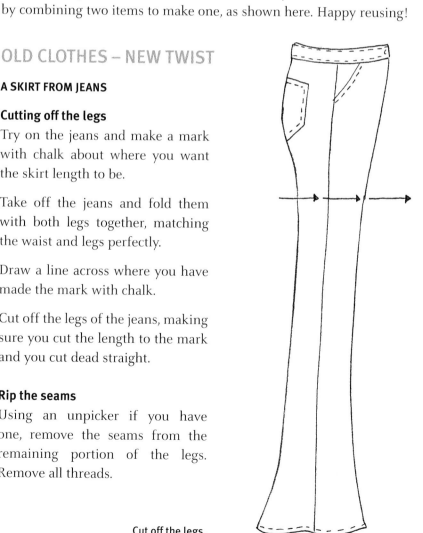

Cut off the legs.

YOU WILL NEED

- A pair of worn jeans (can be ones that are 'gone' in the knee since you will cut the legs off)
- Fabric for a frill (contrasting fabric is best, and one that is softer and easy to drape is better than a stiff fabric like the denim of the jeans)
- Chalk
- Ruler
- Scissors
- Pins
- Tape measure
- Thread (to match the denim or the fabric for the frill, or contrast)
- Unpicker (optional)
- Sewing machine
- Iron and ironing board
- Cloth for pressing

Undo the crotch seam.

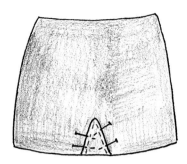

ABOVE **Use a triangular piece of the denim from the legs of the jeans to fill the gap.**

ABOVE RIGHT **Add a frill made from any fabric you wish.**

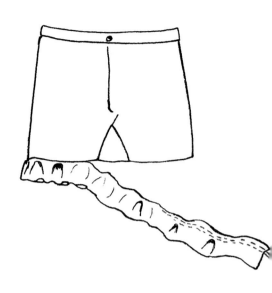

Illustration by Claranick.

Fill the triangular gap

Press flat the flaps that are sticking up, and machine stitch.

Using a piece of denim from the leg of the jeans, cut a triangular piece of fabric that is slightly larger than the gap, and tack in place behind the gap. Machine stitch.

Add the frill

Think first about how you want the frill to look. Choose a contrasting fabric for the frill for a dramatic effect. The sheerer the fabric, the fuller the frill should be. If the frill is wide it needs to be full so that it does not look skimpy, but a narrow frill can be less full.

Cut a strip two to three times the length of the newly created skirt hem, depending on how full you want the frill. If you do not have sufficient fabric, create one long strip by sewing together separate pieces.

Hem the frill for a smart finish or leave it to fray if you prefer.

Sew gathering stitches along the top edge of the frill. Gently ease the fabric along the thread line until the length of the frill matches that of the skirt hem edge.

Pin in place along the bottom edge of the skirt before stitching with a straight or zigzag stitch.

Alternatively, rather than gathering the fabric first, apply the fabric strip by making little folds like pleats, pinning them in place.

Whether you gather or pleat the frill, you will need to sew a seam to join the ends, making the frill one continuous piece, after you have attached the fabric right the way around the hem of the skirt.

TOP TOPS – ADD A FRILL TO THE NECKLINE

A circular frill is best for this. Circular frills can be added to any edge – add one to a cuff for a feminine touch, or to a V-neck or rounded neckline. This method makes a very full, flouncy frill.

The frills need a neatly finished edge to look their best. One option is to make a machine-stitched narrow hem. Do not hem the frill sections until they are all joined together to form the frill. Complete the hem when the pieces are joined, but before the frill is sewn to the fabric it is edging.

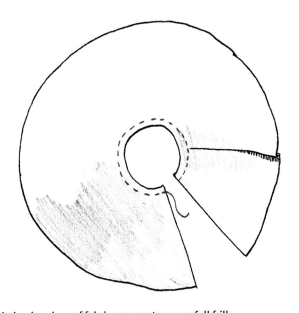

A circular piece of fabric can create a very full frill.

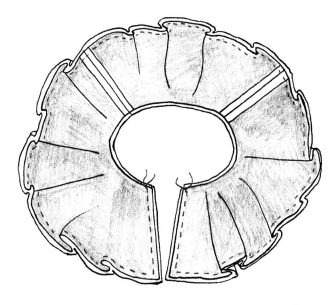

Here pieces are joined to form a circular shape, which is then hemmed around the bottom and also the ends.

For a professional look you can face the entire frill. To make a facing for the frill you can choose to use the same fabric as the frill piece, or a contrasting fabric – this will show a little, so careful selection is required! Cut the facing exactly as you would the frill piece.

Hemmed frill finished with a shaped facing

Cut the frill sections.

Cut a narrow facing that is the shape of the neckline (without the frill).

Join the frill sections together and make a narrow hem around the outer edge.

Pin and then baste the frill to the edge with the wrong side of the frill to the right side of the fabric. Clip the seam allowance up to the line of stitching, clipping especially around deep curves.

With right sides together, pin the facing to the garment edge over the basted frill. The frill is now sandwiched between the two layers. Stitch along the seam line. Trim the seam allowance. Turn the facing to expose the frill.

Press, taking care not to over-press the frill. Hand sew the facing to the garment.

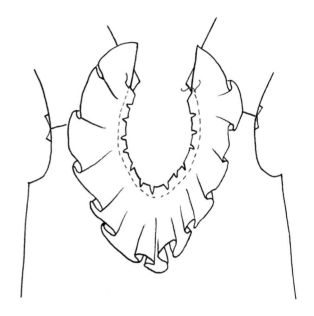

This is the frill applied with the wrong side of the frill against the right side of the garment. To this a small facing will be added to finish the edge off neatly.

Faced frill

Cut the frill sections and cut facings for each frill section.

Join the frill sections together and join the facing sections together.

Stitch the frills to the facings, around the outer edges of the pieces, with right sides together. Turn the frill right side out and press.

Pin and then baste the frill to the neckline on the underside of the garment, with the right side of the frill uppermost. The right side of the frill will be touching the wrong side (inside) of the garment.

Machine stitch into position. Clip the seam allowance up to the line of stitching, clipping at close intervals around deep curves.

Turn the frill to its finished position. Press, taking care not to over-press the frill.

A QUICK WAY OF RUFFLING UP A TOP

YOU WILL NEED

- Fabric for a frill
- V-neck top
- Scissors
- Pins
- Thread and needle
- Sewing machine
- Iron, ironing board, cloth for pressing

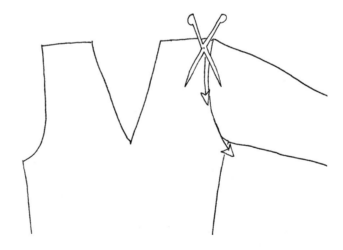

Make the top the shape you wish – maybe cut off the sleeves and hem.

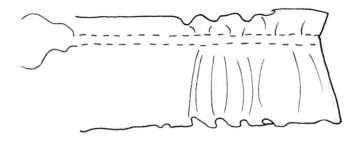

Prepare a narrow frill – this will not cause you too much trouble when applying it! Hem it with a tiny hem.

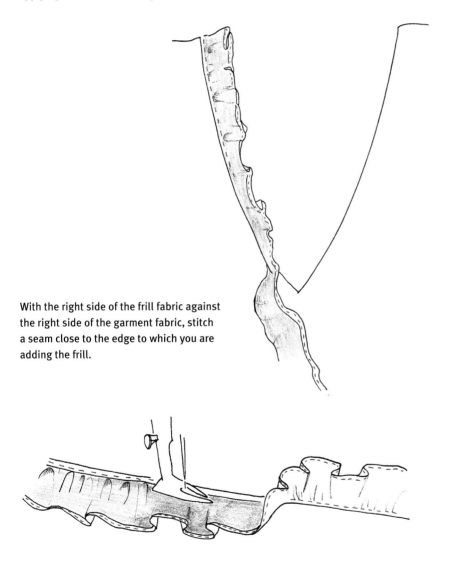

With the right side of the frill fabric against the right side of the garment fabric, stitch a seam close to the edge to which you are adding the frill.

When you have sewn the frill to the garment neck edge, it will flop back down, hiding all the stitching and ruffling nicely – but you may need to give it a gentle press (using a pressing cloth) to encourage it to lie as you want it.

Illustration by Claranick.

CUT A T-SHIRT INTO A BOOB TUBE

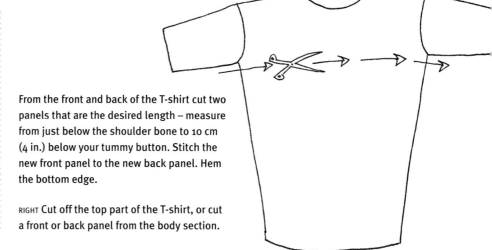

YOU WILL NEED

- ◆ T-shirt
- ◆ Tape measure
- ◆ Chalk
- ◆ Elastic
- ◆ Scissors
- ◆ Pins
- ◆ Thread and needle
- ◆ Sewing machine
- ◆ Iron, ironing board, cloth for pressing

From the front and back of the T-shirt cut two panels that are the desired length – measure from just below the shoulder bone to 10 cm (4 in.) below your tummy button. Stitch the new front panel to the new back panel. Hem the bottom edge.

RIGHT Cut off the top part of the T-shirt, or cut a front or back panel from the body section.

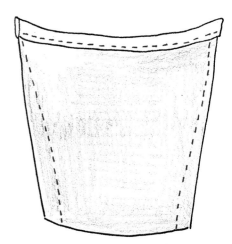

RIGHT Sew the two panels together with right sides together, or if the side seams are still intact you may wish to reshape the top by taking the side seams in a bit for a tighter fit.

At the top edge of the newly formed boob tube, you can either make a casing to put elastic through or stitch a hem before creating a ruched finish.

RIGHT Make a simple casing and thread narrow elastic through.

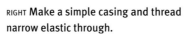

Illustration by Claranick.

To create a ruched finish, use a tiny hand running stitch to sew elastic to the wrong side at the new top edge, pulling the elastic taut as you go. When you let go, the fabric will form little gathers.

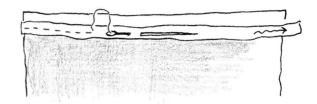

Pull the elastic taut as you sew it to the inside of the top.

It should fit tight to your chest and stay put – but no promises, as it depends on how successful you were at sewing on the elastic while it remained taut. So take note ... and take your time!

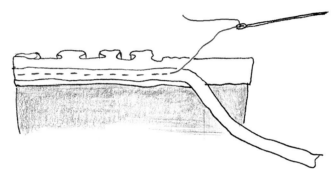

The ruches appear when you let the elastic go after sewing it on.

GO FROM LONG SLEEVES TO A HALTER NECK

YOU WILL NEED

- ◆ V-neck top
- ◆ Scissors
- ◆ Thread and needle
- ◆ Sewing machine
- ◆ Iron, ironing board, cloth for pressing

RIGHT Cut off the sleeves, starting at the armpits towards the neckline. Be sure to cut at an angle that leaves enough fabric over your chest area!

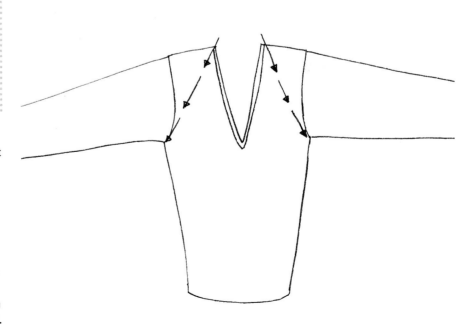

On the back, create a halter neck by cutting a straight line across from one armpit to the other, leaving the neckband intact. Hem all the raw edges with a close zigzag stitch – an overlocker would be great, but not essential.

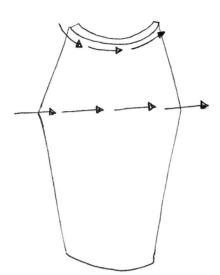

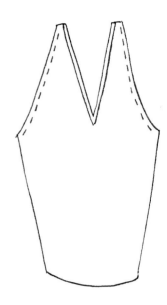

This is the back. You must leave the neckband. Also, do not cut the back too low; cut where the arrows show.

Hem the newly formed armholes.

Hem the newly formed halter neck and back section.

The halter neck creates a top with a totally new shape.

SIMPLE ALTERATIONS

CHANGE THE SHAPE OF TROUSER LEGS

Make a change to trousers and jeans. Taking them in is the obvious choice as it's easy to do – but for fun you could always add godets (see pp.44–5) to flare the legs for a bohemian look. Modify your tight-leg trousers by undoing the seam from the bottom edge to 30 cm (12 in.) up the leg, and inserting a godet of contrasting fabric; it's a good look for Abba fans or fancy dress parties.

Take trousers in, to create straight or skinny legs – if that's the look you like right now. You can do this to trousers or jeans that have a straight leg or a flared leg, but not to trousers that are really wide or baggy.

To taper, or take in tight, lay your jeans or trousers wrong side out with both legs together – one on top of the other – and, measuring from the crotch, draw a line with a long ruler along the inside leg seam for around 30 cm (12 in.). Next, let the line go in at an angle so that the trouser leg will become narrower. Draw the line all the way to the hem at the ankle.

Sew with a machine stitch along this line. After trying on the trousers to make sure it's right, sew along the stitch line a second time in order to reinforce the stitching. Cut off the excess fabric, and use either an overlocker if you have one or a zigzag stitch to neaten the edges.

HEM TROUSERS TO A DIFFERENT LENGTH

To make a trouser leg longer the hem will need to be taken down, and to make the trousers shorter the hem will need to be taken up.

Lengthening trouser legs in five simple steps

1. This is only possible if the hem is not too narrow. Unpick the hem on the trouser legs using an unpicker or scissors. 'Let down' the fabric, by rolling it into place, at a lower level, using your finger and thumb.

2. Pin the trouser legs to the required length. It is best to do this while wearing them to get an accurate result, so ideally get someone to help you with the pinning (mind the pins when you take them off).

3. Use a tacking stitch to secure the hem in its correct position.

4. Press the bottom of the trouser leg, using a cloth between the iron and the trouser. A special sleeve board, which is a narrow board used for pressing seams and garment sections, will make this job easier.

5. Using an invisible hemming stitch, sew the hem of the leg to the trouser leg itself on the inside of the garment. If you want a neat finish inside the trousers, fold over the raw edge as you go.

Shortening trouser legs in five simple steps

1. Unpick the hem on the trouser legs using an unpicker or scissors. 'Roll up' the fabric by rolling it into place at a higher level, using your finger and thumb.

2. Pin the trouser legs to the required length. It is best to do this while they are being worn to get an accurate result, so ideally get someone to help you with the pinning (mind the pins when you take them off).

3. If you are making the trousers considerably shorter, you may need to cut off some of the excess fabric, especially if they are not straight-legged. If you do this, be very careful that you do not cut off too much fabric. Use a tacking stitch to secure the hem in its correct position.

4. Press the bottom of the trouser leg, using a cloth between the iron and the trouser itself. A special sleeve board, which is a narrow board used for pressing seams and garment sections, will make this job easier.

5. Using an invisible hemming stitch, sew the hem of the leg to the trouser leg itself on the inside of the garment. If you want a neat finish inside the trousers, fold over the raw edge as you go.

ADJUST THE SLEEVE LENGTH ON A SHIRT

To shorten a sleeve, remove the cuff or take out the hemming stitches. Remove all threads and press the lower edge flat. Decide on the new sleeve length by trying the shirt on and marking with tailor's chalk or pins. Add a generous hem allowance and make a mark for this below the mark to show the sleeve length. Cut the sleeve shorter just under the hem allowance line. Re-hem the sleeve to the same finish as on the original sleeve.

It is not possible to lengthen a sleeve that has a cuff, but for other sleeves take out the hemming stitches and press the lower edge flat. Turn the hem up by less to allow the sleeve extra length. Re-hem the sleeve to the same finish as on the original sleeve.

SHORTEN A SKIRT OR DRESS AT THE HEM

Try on the garment and ask someone to help you by pinning an even line parallel to the floor, to indicate the new length of the dress. Rip out the original hem and press the fabric flat. Using the pins as a guide, fold up the hem to the desired length. Press along the fold. Mark a line 6 cm (2¼ in.) below this fold, which will become the stitching line. Cut along the line. Re-hem the garment using the fold as a guide and using the same finish as on the original dress.

If there is a back pleat on the skirt or dress, shorten the pleat in the same way as the hem if it will be longer than 10 cm (4 in.) when finished. If the pleat will become shorter than 10 cm (4 in.) when finished, stitch it shut completely and lose the feature, as it will look odd if it is too short.

LENGTHEN A SKIRT OR DRESS AT THE HEM

Rip out the original hem and press the fabric flat. In some cases there will be enough fabric to let down – if so, pin your new hem in position before basting it and hemming it to the same finish as was featured on the original dress. If there is not enough fabric to let down, you will need to add a facing. Skirt facings must be cut on the bias and it is best to use matching fabric if possible, or at least fabric of a similar weight and colour.

Start at a seam and pin the facing to the lower edge of the skirt with right sides together. Stitch the facing to the skirt and press open the seam. Turn the facing to the inside and baste along the folded edge. Working on the inside of the garment, make a hem on the facing to neaten the edge, turning the hem under to the wrong side of the skirt. Slip stitch the facing to the skirt.

You can also add length to a lightweight skirt by adding a band of lace. This is lapped over the lower edge of the skirt and hand stitched in place.

SHORTEN A SKIRT FROM THE WAISTLINE

A skirt that has a decorative detail at the lower edge can be shortened by raising from the waistline instead of at the hem. Remove or unpick the waistband, zip and darts, and then remove the band at the top of the skirt. Try on the skirt and pin where the new darts should be placed to ensure a good fit over the hips. Stitch the new darts and replace the zip and waistband.

TAKE IN THE WAIST AND HIPS ON A SKIRT OR DRESS

For a skirt or dress that is too big, first try on the garment wrong side out, and pin away some of the bulk of the fabric at the seams. Take off the dress and use a basting stitch to make a seam that tapers into the old seam line. Make sure you adjust the skirt by the same amount at each side. Try it on again before stitching a permanent seam. If you need to take out the zip in order to make this adjustment, reinsert it in the same way as it was originally put in. Press open new seams and remove the old stitching after sewing your new seams.

LET OUT THE WAIST AND HIPS ON A SKIRT

For a skirt that is too tight, open the seams using an unpicker and press the seams together. Determine how much fabric can be let out, and pin and baste each side seam so that they allow an equal amount of fullness. The seam should start at the waist and should taper towards the hip. The stitching should continue down to join the side seam at the lower edge of the skirt. If you need to take out the zip in order to make this adjustment, reinsert it in the same way as it was originally put in. Press open new seams and remove the old stitching after sewing your new seams.

REPLACE A BROKEN ZIP

There is no cheat way of mending a broken zip – you need to buy a replacement one that is the same length, weight and colour as the original. Remove the old zip with an unpicker or scissors, and pull out all the threads. Press the old seams open and insert the new zip in the same way in which the original one was applied.

Even if making a garment from start to finish is not for you, it is great to be able to repair and remodel your clothes. There are many things you can do to make clothes you have bought fit better too. Simple alterations as well as total makeovers can give your wardrobe new life.

Whether you are mending, altering or making, enjoy creating something new with fabric. Happy sewing!

Use fabric paints, appliqué and embellishments such as beads and sequins to create a fabric surface that is unique. This dress, by Georgia Fernley, is made from cotton that has been decorated with rose motifs using different textile techniques.

Glossary

basting   loose, temporary stitching used in the preparatory stages of assembling a garment or item

bias   the diagonal direction of fabric (which runs at 45 degrees to the grain line)

bias binding   a strip used to encase edges as a finish or trim, which is cut on the bias of the fabric

casing   a channel formed either by folding an extended edge or by sewing on an additional strip, which houses elastic or a drawstring made from braid or ribbon

collar stand   the band (usually interfaced) on to which a tailored shirt collar is sewn

facing   a fitted piece of fabric that is sewn on the raw edge of a garment and turned under to give a clean finish

grading   the trimming of layers of fabric to different widths, to reduce bulk on seam allowances

grain line   the direction of the threads in a woven fabric

grosgrain   silk fabric or ribbon with a crosswise texture

hem   a finish at an edge of fabric, made by folding the raw edge under and stitching it down

lining   a concealed layer of fabric that lines the outer layer to preserve shape, add body, or create comfort

mitre   a diagonal join where two hems meet at a corner

notches   small wedges cut from the seam allowance to reduce bulk. Also a pattern symbol used to indicate where pieces must match up during assembly; notches should be transferred to the fabric when cutting out

pinking shears   scissors with a scalloped edge that creates a zigzag cut, which helps prevent fraying along raw edges of fabric

raw edge   unfinished edge of fabric

Make something that no one else has – this patchwork cushion is made from fabric swatches.

seam   a row of stitches to hold sections of fabric together

self-facing   of the same material as the rest of the garment

selvedge   the narrow, flat, woven border found at both lengthwise
                  sides of fabric

tacking   a long, loose, temporary hand stitch used to join two
                  layers together

Dyed cotton lace dresses a window
beautifully. Sew a casing and then hem
with care.

Index

These vintage embroideries and lace fabrics make a gorgeous bedspread.

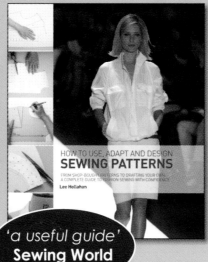